this human

design character

Know who you are as a designer.

MELIS SENOVA, PhD

BIS Publishers
Borneostraat 80-A
1094 CP Amsterdam
The Netherlands
T +31 (0)20 515 02 30
bis@bispublishers.com
www.bispublishers.com

ISBN 978-90-6369-652-8

Category: Design / Personal Development / Leadership

Design and Layout by Karina Northover and Tayla Farrugia
Reviewed by Annie Clarke and Cyndi Dawes
Illustrated by Melis Senova

All web references were correct at the time of going to press.

To those,
mostly unseen,
who shape
the experience
of this world.

Who know
to design
is a moral act.

Who are ready to embrace
the responsibility that comes
with designing our future.

TABLE OF CONTENTS

ACKNOWLEDGEMENTS

DEAR READER

Every person mentioned here volunteered on this project. They gave up their precious time to support me in this endeavour, simply because they believe in me and in this work. It is because of their commitment that this book is now before you.

DEAR KARINA

You were unfaltering in your support of me and this work. You are a dear friend and a respected colleague. The magic you weave to bring the copy and illustrations to life is inspiring. You took the egg image and turned it into a book! I continue to learn so much from you. Because you haven't heard it enough in the past year, thank you thank you thank you.

DEAR TAYLA

Look what you did! The amount of work you put into laying out this book is unspeakable. You are just at the beginning of what I know will be the most exciting and varied career. You have many feathers to your cap already my friend, and you can add a whole book to it now. You are a thoughtful, considerate and great designer Tayla, I can't wait to see what you do next.

DEAR CYNDI

Is there anything we can't do together? I don't think so. Our adventures have been many and varied and we can add a book to the long list. You are always in support of me and my work, always. Thank you for your discerning eye, your rapid and honest reviews, the subtle grammar lessons and for believing in me.

DEAR LJ

Through the whirlwind that has been 2022, you showed up and dove in to whatever needed attention. From creating our business strategy to our content calendars, from reaching out to academics to creating the resources and reference list. You did it all. You are a wonder, and I am so happy you are here with me on this adventure.

DEAR ANNIE

Here we are again! We did it! You are a loyal friend and colleague, thank you for stepping in where you could to help bring another creation into the world. In amongst the craziness of life and writing your own book, you continue to show up with your beautiful smile and golden heart. Thank you dearest Annie.

DEAR ZAANA

I am so grateful you agreed to write the Foreword I will never forget your response when I asked you, it was so beautiful. Rather than share it here, I'll leave it as a story for you to tell. Having your insightful, experienced and wise words as a part of this book is a gift, and I know how important they are to current and future generations of designers. Thank you.

DEAR MUM AND DAD

The last year has been a lot to handle for both of you. Despite this, you both find it within yourself to pull out those pom poms and cheer me all the way to the finish line. You always have, and always will. I love you both.

DEAR CHARLIE

You were by my side, every... single... moment. You teach me about loyalty and love every day. Thanks for being there for me when everyone else was sleeping, and wagging your tail when I was too tired to wag my own.

DEAR CAM

There were a few early starts and a few stressful moments and a renewed understanding of why there were five years between books. You make sure life keeps ticking while my attention is elsewhere, in your quiet, gentle, supportive and ever present way. Thank you for being there for me again, and again, and again.

DEAR COOPER

You probably think you didn't really do anything to help me write this book, but that is so far from the truth. You focussed on your studies, took care of everything that needed to happen in your world, and gave me the time and space to create this work. Your contribution is immense in that regard. I am so grateful to have you in my life, even though I put you in it. Thank you.

Foreword

We need more dialogue on the essential capabilities designers require in this metamodern age, to be conscious and responsible for what they put out in the world and the impact they create. Over the past 15 years, design has lived through the hype cycle of business vernacular and earned its 'seat at the table'. From a design capability perspective it has moved from focusing primarily on the tools and processes of design to integrate design mindsets.

THIS BOOK IS AN INVITATION AND INITIATION INTO THE NEXT STAGE OF MATURITY IN DESIGN CAPABILITY—THAT OF DESIGN CHARACTER.

Bill O'Brien, former CEO Hanover Insurance stated *"The success of an intervention depends on the interior condition of the intervener."* The same is true for design—the success or quality of a design depends on the interior condition of the designer. This interior condition is the character Melis is asking us to inquire into.

Design is being increasingly democratised through its accessibility and uptake of tools and methods. While this is important for the inclusivity, accessibility and maturity of both the discipline and design outcomes, it has often come at the cost of impact. High impact design outcomes require a specific set of conditions. As I learned through my PhD research, it is dependent on maturity across three dimensions:

1. The environment for design (both within the team and the system);
2. The approach taken; and the
3. Designer/s themselves.

THE MORE DESIGNERS UNDERSTAND AND DO THE WORK ON THEMSELVES THE MORE THEY ARE ABLE TO UNDERSTAND OTHERS.

By nature of design being a creative process, you can't remove the designer —and therefore their character—from influencing the outcome of design. Give 100 designers the same design challenge and you will get 100 different solutions of varying quality. While this is understood, there is little consideration for the impact of the designer on the quality or success of design outcomes, trusting instead that the approach will deliver. *We've effectively tried to democratise the designer out of design when the designer is the lynchpin.*

To build on this further, my research found that maturity of the designer occurs across two axes; *their technical capability in design, and their mindset of how they view and approach design.* What I've come to learn in the decade since is the important third dimension —*the character of the designer.*

Those who work on their interior condition inevitably are able to facilitate more impactful design outcomes. Why? Because design character also forms part of self leadership, and self leadership is the first intervention to successfully influence and lead teams, then organisations and systems.

Further, they are able to navigate polarities in increasingly complex environments. They bring the ability to 'Look AT' a person, problem or situation objectively, to observe it without judgement or bias, see the multiplicity of perspectives at play, and appreciate the complexity and diversity of needs. They are also able to 'Look AS' a person, to truly step into having empathy and compassion for what is happening internally, what it's like to be that person, problem, or in that situation. All of this supports being able to hold both 'Looking AT' and 'Looking AS' in perspective to get the optimal balance of positive design outcomes with minimal unintended consequences for the actors involved.

This metamodern era is also calling for a new paradigm of leadership. Designers have been at the forefront of the mindsets of this new paradigm for the past decade, drawing attention to empathy, experimentation, diversity and collaboration. The rest of the world is catching up. Because designers naturally embody the mindsets of design—and in so doing the mindsets of this new leadership paradigm—this can be mistaken for having done the work on character. However, mindsets don't necessarily translate into character.

For example from a practice perspective, I have witnessed people with these mindsets bring in personal biases and design products and services based on their perspectives instead of customer needs. From a leadership perspective, I have seen designers ignore power imbalances that can cause anxiety and trauma, and expect their teams to be 'authentic' yet not create the psychological safety for them to do so.

I've also seen designers themselves and those around them overestimate their capability and risk causing harm or negative consequences through not considering the elements of design character—particularly values, ethics, power, safety, boundaries and self-care.

If a project requires something a little outside the norm, it's often taken on by a designer because it's seen as requiring more creative problem solving and resembles what designers do. This might involve complex stakeholder engagement, creative workshops to navigate relationships and systems, and engaging people on change. These all require specialist skills such as community engagement, partnership brokerage, masterful facilitation, and change management. These situations can cause harm often stemming from naivety, overconfidence or over-responsibility in designers.

We would all benefit from paying greater respect to adjacent skills and disciplines as well as developing our design character. This would take us forward into the next horizon of design maturity by looking inward at ourselves and inquiring "Who am I" to be designing?

In design, it is critical to bring discussion about power, ethics, safety, self-care and boundaries to the forefront. We are increasingly being asked to be advocates for, and leaders in, these topics for our organisations and communities. As a result, we need to be more responsible in our practice.

We need to understand the intended and unintended consequences of our designs, methods and approaches—on ourselves, other humans and the more than human actors involved. Getting focused on a solution or method without thinking through the full extent of the impact or consequences is no longer acceptable.

This work on design character— understanding who you are and how you show up in your work—while framed within the context of design, is timely and transferable more broadly to leadership character, or simply your character full stop. Regardless of context, developing your character is a self-development journey and a life work. It requires a preparedness and readiness to look at yourself, understand who you are and what informs you in all the shades of light and shadow; a willingness to question what you perceive to be true; a desire to learn and grow through experimentation; and a compassion and kindness for yourself and others.

The ***Design Character framework*** provides a foundation for you to commence this journey. Particularly if you're new to self-work and character development, framing it within one context like design can be helpful to provide focus and specificity for you to think through the concepts, and experiment within familiar boundaries.

But know that the application of design character will have ripple effects in your life beyond design. It will support you not only in growing your capability and impact as a designer but also your growth as a human.

DR. ZAANA HOWARD

Dr Zaana Howard has 15+ years of global experience in human-centred design, leadership development, and organisational culture and change. She is the Founder and Director of Camino, a practice focused on transformational transitions to support individuals, teams and organisations in becoming more conscious, connected and compassionate. Previously, Zaana was a Junior Partner at McKinsey & Company driving human-centric transformations for public, social and health services. She holds a PhD in Design from Swinburne University.

Preface

WHY I *wrote* THIS BOOK

As I sat down at my desk, staring at an empty manuscript document, I wondered again why I was writing this book. I had been here before. Contemplating the very same question as when I began writing the first book in this series. *This human: how to be the person designing for other people* was created to shine the light on practices that are important and relevant to nurture a sustainable way of being while designing.

This book has a similar purpose, but with more focus, stronger energy and greater sense of urgency. It is designed to catalyse deeper dives, which can be the impetus to rethink, reframe and respond to a thorough understanding of yourself, and of design itself.

We all need a little more space in our lives to ask the simple and important questions. You know the ones—those we typically avoid. The questions we sometimes seek help to answer; whether it's with a therapist, a friend, a partner, a lover, a tree or a deck of oracle cards. Who am I? Why am I here? What rights/beliefs/emotions am I fundamentally entitled to? Am I seeking meaning and purpose? How and where do I find them? What does it all mean?

Humility prevents me from stating that you'll find the answers to these ancient questions within the pages of this book, but I am confident you will know more about yourself and why you design the way you do by the end of it. You will also realise why knowing yourself is fundamental to design, and see how knowing 'who' is doing the designing is critical to expanding and deepening your design practice in important and impactful ways.

TOO MUCH OF WHAT WE DESIGN IS UNCONSCIOUS.

When I use the word unconscious, I don't really mean it in its literal sense. If you are at work, and you are talking to people, moving a mouse around and making decisions, clearly you are conscious (most of the time).

What I mean is, we don't always consider the implications of our actions holistically, or with an eye on the longer-term horizon, or with an internal compass that says, 'yep, I'm okay with this' or 'nope, not ok with this'. There are often too many competing requirements to hold all this in our minds while trying to get projects out the door, right? This is where the challenge lies.

In the absence of this clarity, we can be at the whim of more powerful voices, better articulated goals and tighter timeframes, even when those voices, goals and timeframes make our own bodies feel constricted and heavy. Without literacy in our own values, we don't necessarily know why we are feeling dissonance with our work, and the way we are professionally trained makes us comply with what is expected of us. We get paid for the work and if we've met the brief, we get a pat on the back. But we've lost something in the process. A little bit of us has faded; perhaps our morals, perhaps our integrity, perhaps our passion.

This book is about equipping you with the awareness of what makes you tick, in a way that is relevant to what you do as a designer. *Knowledge and awareness of who you are helps build resilience to the forces that might expect you to design something that you otherwise wouldn't.* Like the first book, this book is intended to be your life-long companion. One that will, like you, remain relevant and age gracefully.

THE WORLD NEEDS MORE BALANCE.

It is a privilege to sit in a comfortable room, on a comfortable chair, in a safe place and share my perspective with the world. And it is my perspective, completely. This work is an expression of my experience of living. And with that framing, from where I sit, I see a world of people who value what can be perceived with the five primary senses; what can be measured directly, what makes money, what brings power and creates influence. What I don't see, in equal measure, is a world of people who value deep contemplation, diversity and backstory. One that is curious about all it cannot perceive or measure directly, or one that values vulnerability and the wisdom to know when to yield, and rest, and pause.

This focus is symptomatic of left-brain dominance. This is important to note, because the right brain tends to care about the inter-relatedness of things, it has a huge tolerance for ambiguity and not knowing, and it can process complexity very quickly because it doesn't waste time breaking things down into its separate parts (McGilchrist, 2009).

In this book, the topics we cover are not explicit, we concern ourselves with what is often implicit. Values cannot be directly perceived by our five senses, nor can we weigh them on a scale, but they direct our attention and inform our motivation. And as designers, we need to know what is at work within ourselves, so we understand the backstory of what we put out there in the world. This self-knowledge helps us ask new questions, direct our attention to novel places and accept differing perspectives. This is where our potential lives.

So, this book is another endeavour to bring more awareness and reflexivity to your work as designers. I feel so passionately about this global community of world-builders and creators. It is through the act of creation and design that things that once didn't exist come into being. The Earth, our shared home, is at a critical time in its existence, and we put it there, with our creations and our designs. This book will help you have more clarity about what you put out there in the world. Once you know what's informing your design judgements and directing your attention, you can also question whether it is appropriate. You can better discern the best action, given who you are now, and the time you are living in.

This is a contribution I know I can make. It is one I do with love, hope and sense of service, and always a dash of humour.

Introduction

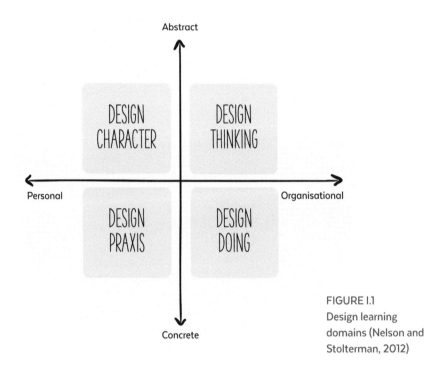

FIGURE I.1
Design learning
domains (Nelson and
Stolterman, 2012)

WHAT *is* DESIGN CHARACTER?

One part of why this book exists is to fill a gap I see in design education. In my view, the intention of design education is to teach individuals how to 'become designers', rather than 'do design'. To teach this we need a holistic understanding of what it is to be a designer. Luckily, Nelson and Stolterman (2012) have already done a lot of the heavy lifting for us. I will use their work as a basis to explain design character and the gap it fills.

Designers require a set of competencies to grow into design completely. These competencies can be understood as mindsets, knowledge sets, skill sets and tool sets (Nelson and Stolterman, 2012). Each contributes to a different domain of development which can be explained elegantly in the above framework.

Due to the current orientation of what we value as a society, which I alluded to in the Preface, we tend to focus on things external to us and concrete in nature. So much of our focus has been on teaching design doing and more recently on design thinking. Both of these domains of learning are critical and essential, but currently our focus is swayed in this direction, and this leaves a gap.

Moving our focus internally, and remaining in the concrete space, we find ourselves in the domain of Design Praxis—the process of transmuting knowledge into action. The way I distinguish between design praxis and design doing is that the former is about the designer's skill, the latter is the application of this skill using design tools. In this way, you can see that one is internal (personal) and the other is external (organisational).

Design character refers to the internal conditions that inform every other learning domain. It is a designer's core.

"No judgment made by a designer can be made solely based on comprehensive knowledge. [Design] judgments always depend on the designer's core values... The designer has to believe in their capacity to make good judgements... grounded in the roots of their character." Nelson and Stolterman, 2012.

This means we need a way to work with this character—your design character. We need to know what it is, and continue to develop and cultivate it. This is what this work is about. It is about providing scaffolding for your evolving and unfolding values, ethics and praxis, as you become, and are, a designer.

DESIGN CHARACTER WORK ENABLES YOU TO DESIGN THE DESIGNER.

01

VALUES

Our values direct our attention and motivate our behaviour. Knowing yours will help you understand what you are naturally drawn towards *(and away from)* in your work.

This chapter is a
guided encounter
with your own
values and the
part they play in
how you design.

WE START WITH VALUES.

We start with values because they
sit in the background and direct your
attention, influence the meaning you
make and the actions you take. Knowing
them helps you understand why you
like certain types of design, contexts for
design and specific methods and tools.
Knowing them also gives you pointers
as to where else you might need to more
actively direct attention.

What are values?

My fascination and love for the human condition, in all its muck and glory, is deep and long-standing. I am interested in what is under the surface, what is really driving our thoughts, emotions and behaviours. Because I'm a designer and a neuroscientist, I've always stepped humbly in the field of psychology and it is with that humility that I present my research on values.

When researching this chapter and the content for my course, Design Character, I looked for a framework that was applicable to many contexts, one that was universal. I wanted to create a space for us all to discuss values in general, using common language, and to gain insight into our own values and the way they play out in our work.

Design Character is about understanding who you are as a designer and how you show up in your design work.

Your values are the background upon which your design character tapestry is woven.

Your values influence where your attention is naturally drawn, and the meaning you make from the experiences you have.

One of the challenges I've faced in my career was how to situate myself within what I was doing and where I was doing it. Let me explain. When I use that word 'situate', what I'm really talking about is being able to discern whether what I am doing is aligned with who I know myself to be. I've always experienced this as a feeling. If there was alignment, it felt good; if there wasn't alignment, it didn't. And most of the time this was enough for me to listen to and act upon, but to be honest it felt more intuitive than well thought out.

What I'd been doing was checking in with my values. It took reflection and work to realise that's what was happening and it's why I'm so passionate about sharing this learning with you.

In my exploration for a common framework I came across the Schwartz Theory of Basic Values (Schwartz, 2012). The following characteristics of values struck me as a good basis upon which to have robust and meaningful conversation with others about our values, using common language.

SUMMARY OF WHAT VALUES ARE ACCORDING TO SCHWARTZ (AND ME).

Values are emotional

Emotions are typically asked to take a back seat in our work. We need to learn how to work with emotional responses to guide our thinking and actions consciously.

Values motivate action

They are linked to our desirable goals. Knowing why we have the goals we do helps us manage why we are drawn to certain outcomes and not others.

Values are agnostic of context

This is what sets them apart from norms, and why they are culturally pervasive. Knowing this is an important framework for yourself, but also for your work. Designers work with values all the time.

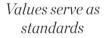

Values serve as standards

They set up an intrinsic guide against which you measure your actions and that of others. Understanding the motivations behind others' actions makes you an insightful designer.

Values are relative

The importance of values change depending on the situation you are in. They can be in conflict or they can be in support. They exist inside of you, and are present between people. Knowing how to navigate this is essential to great design.

These really spoke to me.

As designers, being literate in our own values enables us to be clear about how our orientation shapes our interpretation of the work we do. Sometimes it is important for us to focus purely on connecting with another's perspective, being as neutral and open as possible. For instance, when we are learning and researching how others are in the world and how they experience systems, services or products.

Other times, when we are at delivery stage and advocating for people or the work, we need to be present fully with all our own world views, values and ethical frameworks to stand strong in them.

In these moments, if we are not clear, we are at risk of either putting something into the world that we didn't intend, or of being swayed by the clearer, more present values of others, that may not necessarily be our own. As designers, as people who create experiences and realities for others, this is risky.

Next we'll go deeper into Schwartz's Theory where you'll get an opportunity to work out what your values are by using an amazing survey created by the University of Western Australia.

The Schwartz Values Circumplex

Students who have studied Design Character will know how much I love a circumplex; say it three times out loud. Go on. It's satisfying isn't it? The best way to engage with this section of the chapter is to complete the values survey (https://www.thevaluesproject.com) for yourself (it doesn't take too long) and then you'll be able to reflect on your results.

You'll get more out of the next part of this book if you do the survey. So, stop reading now and do it. I'll still be here when you come back.

Schwartz undertook a study to create a model that expressed universal, shared human values. His aim was to unearth and share values that cross cultures, ethnicities, geographies and perhaps even generations. It was no mean feat.

While spending some time in the land of values research and analysis, I found that many other researchers referred back to, or leveraged, this model in one form or another. I find it useful for what we are here to learn about.

The thing about this model that helps us shed light on how values operate, is not the values as individual values, but the way they interact together across the wheel (or circumplex). Their locations are significant but I don't need to go into too much detail except to say if they are next to each other, they are closely related; if they are on the opposite side of the wheel; they are not.

This is relevant because as a person, it is common for us to have two values, both primary, on opposite sides of the wheel. For example, you may have self-direction and conformity as equally strong values. The experience of this in your life would be the tension you feel, normally somewhere in your body, about wanting to do things your way and keeping other people happy.

"*I have learned that as long as I hold fast to my beliefs and values—and follow my own moral compass—then the only expectations I need to live up to are my own.*"

Michelle Obama

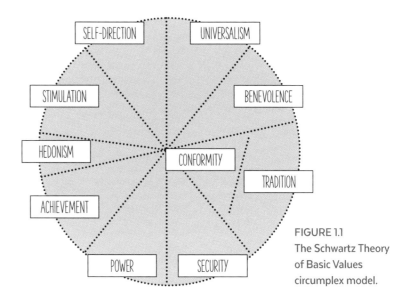

THE SCHWARTZ THEORY OF BASIC VALUES CIRCUMPLEX MODEL

These definitions are from the website shared earlier with some additional keywords from the paper by Schwartz.

FIGURE 1.1
The Schwartz Theory of Basic Values circumplex model.

SELF-DIRECTION

Self-direction values are about thinking and acting independently. For people who value self-direction highly, it is very important to be free to choose their own goals and actions and to rely upon themselves. They want to learn and explore different topics and ways of thinking and to be original and creative.

Key terms: creativity, freedom, choosing own goals, curiosity, independence.

STIMULATION

Stimulation values are about seeking new and exciting things to do. For people who value stimulation highly, it is very important to live an exciting life filled with variety and novelty. They enjoy change and adventure and like to try lots of new things. They tend to seek thrilling experiences.

Key terms: variety, excitement, adventure, daring.

HEDONISM

Hedonism values are about seeking pleasure and enjoyment in life. For people who value hedonism highly, it is very important to enjoy life's pleasures, to have fun and indulge themselves. They want to relax, enjoy and pamper themselves.

Key terms: pleasure, indulgence, satisfaction, enjoyment.

ACHIEVEMENT

Achievement values are about seeking success according to social standards. It is very important to be ambitious, achieve goals and show capability and competence. They want to succeed in life and get ahead. They seek to influence and impress others and to be recognised for their success.

Key terms: ambition, success, influence, capability, social recognition.

POWER

Power values are about seeking to control people and resources. For people who value power highly, control and wealth are important. They want the authority or power to dominate others. Being rich and having high status is important.

Key terms: authority, wealth, social power.

SECURITY

Security values are about being safe personally and living in a secure and stable society. It is very important to avoid any danger, risk or uncertainty. To live in a well-ordered, predictable environment, they want their society to be safe for their family and others, with a government that can protect them against threats.

Key terms: moderate, safe, healthy, social order, national security.

CONFORMITY

Conformity values are about adhering to rules and to others' expectations. For people who value conformity highly, it is very important to follow rules and regulations and to meet all their obligations. They want to behave properly and to avoid upsetting others. They want to be polite and to avoid doing anything people would say is wrong.

Key terms: obedience, self-discipline, honour, self-restraint, etiquette.

TRADITION

Tradition values are about following cultural and religious traditions. For people who value tradition highly, it is very important to maintain, observe and respect the traditional practices, ideas and ways of thinking of their family, religion or ethnic group.

Key terms: respect, commitment, humility, responsiveness to expectation.

BENEVOLENCE

Benevolence values are about caring for people you are close to, your family and friends. For people who value benevolence highly, it is very important to put the welfare of their family and friends ahead of their own. It is important for them to be helpful, responsible and dependable.

Key terms: helpful, honest, forgiving, responsible, loyal, caring.

UNIVERSALISM (SOCIETAL)

Universalism-societal values are about wanting everyone to have equal opportunities in life. For people who value universalism-societal highly, the welfare of all the people in the world is very important. They want to understand and accept people who are different from themselves and to help people who have less than themselves.

UNIVERSALISM (NATURE)

Universalism-nature values are about caring for the natural environment and for all animals. For people who value universalism-nature highly, it is critical to protect the environment from pollution and destruction. It is important for them to preserve the water, land, air, plants and animals for future generations.

Key terms: understanding, acceptance, tolerance, coherence, holistic thought relating to society and nature.

I also want to name Spirituality as a value, although Schwartz excludes it from this list because his study was about defining universal/shared human values, he found Spirituality values differed too much across cultures to fill that criteria. But for our purposes in this book, I think it is worth a mention, again, based on his research.

SPIRITUALITY

Spirituality values are about connecting to meaning in life, experiencing coherence and inner harmony through transcendence or deep acceptance of everyday reality. The values would be derived from the need to find ultimate meaning in one's experience of life. For people who value spirituality highly, it is important to connect to something greater than oneself, to feel unity with all things and to be devout in their spiritual practice.

Key terms: faith, connection, ritual, unity.

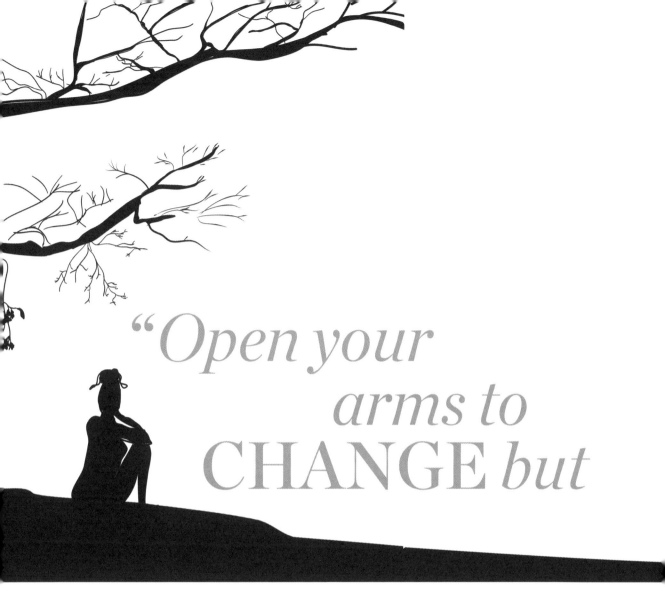

"Open your arms to CHANGE but don't let go of your VALUES."

Dalai Lama

Why are values important?

Now that we've got the basics down, you're probably wondering why we are spending time with this model.

It is a foundation piece of information we'll keep coming back to for the next few chapters. It's foundational because values direct our attention and influence our motivation.

As designers, we need to know where our attention naturally flows, because what we attend to, we tend to create and bring into the world. What doesn't have our attention doesn't get created. It's extremely important for you to know your values, so you know what you're NOT paying attention to. We'll talk more about this connection in Chapter 2.

In this chapter we're going to focus on the experience of understanding your own values and how that then affects your design character.

Ooh, thrilling!

By the end of this book you will have built a Design Character framework, which is a living document, helping you constantly refine and create your design character to have potency and influence in your world.

Knowing your values helps you make decisions about the type of design you'd like to practice and where you'd like to practice it. In this chapter we're consolidating our understanding of ourselves as designers within the framework of the *values circumplex.*

So let's unpack why values are important in the context of design work.

YES!
I WORKED
IT IN AGAIN.

1. VALUES DIRECT
your ATTENTION

What we value has importance to us, and our attention is typically drawn towards what we place value on. As a designer, your attention takes the form of design thinking and action. The most important aspect of this is to understand what is not in view.

What are you not paying attention to because it is not something you place value on? This is a key reflection that needs to be incorporated into how you design. It goes some way to ensuring your practice is one that strives towards compensating for the embedded prejudice and bias in the systems we operate within.

2. VALUES DIRECT
your PRIORITIES

There are moments in the design process where we make decisions and judgements. Imagine you've just finished a body of design research. You are in a room full of data, some already up on the walls and some stuck in online tools.

There will be types of data you are naturally drawn to, that you feel comfortable working with. There will also be questions or stories you feel are irrelevant.

Knowing how you are oriented as a designer will give you the mindedness to discern whether you need to make more effort to look in places you wouldn't normally, to ask questions that might seem boring or irrelevant.

For example, one of my values is universalism, both social and environment rank highly. That means my attention is usually drawn toward large systemic topics and impacts. The task in front of me may be to fix a single point of pain for a citizen, but my attention will be naturally drawn towards trying to solve it for the whole system.

I will be fascinated by the interconnected nature of things, the between spaces, the gaps and transitions in experiences, but not necessarily on the actual experience itself. Knowing this about how my attention is normally directed, I have learnt how to direct it towards things I normally wouldn't, or feel resistance towards. This encourages a richer consideration set in my work.

3. VALUES DEFINE *your* STANDARDS

Knowing your values helps you also discern what is ok and what is not. Having this clarity builds confidence to speak about your views and perspectives. Your values will define the standards you have around process, tools, skill sets, interactions and outcomes.

For example, if one of your values is benevolence, you might prefer participatory and trauma-informed design methods as they have care and consideration embedded into them.

If your value is stimulation, you might be drawn to the latest methods and have an experimental approach to design. If your value is conformity, you might choose to adopt what the organisation already has in place in subtle yet effective ways, rather than bringing in something completely different.

There is no right or wrong, better or worse. The whole point is to know who you are in the context of your work so you can own your practice and also make deliberate deviations where appropriate.

4. VALUES DEFINE *your* BEHAVIOURS

One graduate of the Design Character course, has a primary value of benevolence. She became aware that the need to look after family and friends extends to her work colleagues, as she sees them as her work family. She will work outside of hours to ensure her team needs are always met. Her new awareness enabled the correction of her behaviour and brought more balance to how she worked.

For example, there may be a person in your team who leaps to new ideas, seemingly not interested to settle on any concept to develop it further. They may be constantly challenging the norms of the organisation, or the boundaries and scope of the project. This person may have strong stimulation and self-direction values.

Knowing this about your colleague brings a sense of understanding to their behaviour. Rather than getting frustrated, there may be other ways to direct their attention towards the things you can see that they cannot. This is the beauty of building diverse teams.

5. VALUES INFORM *your* MEANING MAKING

There is a story my mother tells me from her teaching days. One of her mentors said, "there will be an incident in the classroom and every student will witness it, but each student will have a slightly different retelling of it."

How we make meaning of what we notice and the way we then express that meaning is all influenced by our values, our personalities and our life experiences. Having the skills and awareness to reflect and critique the meaning you are making about an interaction with a citizen or a customer, a colleague or your boss is an essential capability. It gives you access to the space you need as a designer to check for your own biases, to interrogate your own thinking about whether where you have arrived is actually a fair representation of what was shared.

This is particularly important when the people you are designing with have completely disparate life experiences and contexts to your own. We all reflect our own realities on each other and other people's experiences. The fact is that everyone experiences life in a unique way. Our role as designers is to get as close as we possibly can to understanding another's reality so we can design with empathy and deep understanding of their experience, not our own. This can only be present if you are aware of the types of filters you have operating, so you can do your best to understand their influence.

A little story...

I have run this exercise with many groups now, and there is always a sense of awkwardness that occurs when people are surprised about one of their values.

One particular student realised that Power was a primary value. She was quite resistant to that at first. She did not like the experience of someone behaving in a dominant way, nor did she like that perhaps she might be motivated by social status or accumulation of wealth.

However, values are inert, in that a value in its own right is not good or bad, it is not right or wrong. What actually matters is the way your values are enacted.

When reminded of this, she saw the most important aspect of the framework (circumplex), is the interrelatedness of the values. She also had universalism as one of her stronger values and seeing the interplay between power and universalism had her transmute those feelings of resistance into a deeper understanding of how she wants to express herself in the world.

GETTING TO KNOW YOUR OWN VALUES.

This exercise helps you become familiar with your own values so you have a benchmark to keep referring back to.

UNIVERSALISM

01 DO THE SURVEY

Follow The Values Project link provided in this chapter and in the Resources and complete the values survey (if you haven't already).

02 CREATE YOUR VALUES SUMMARY

I've included mine as an example on the next page. The size of the bubble in the outputs reflects its relative importance. Click on each of the bubbles in order of size and make a note of the value and its short description. I've arranged mine in three columns, you're welcome to do the same.

03 REFLECT ON YOUR VALUES

Use the following questions to unpack how you feel about your values.

1. What did you notice when you first received your results?
2. Which values are you proud of ?
3. Which values are you resistant to?
4. For both 2. and 3., why do you think this is?
5. What do you think is missing?

REMEMBER

THIS IS A SNAPSHOT. YOU ARE A PERSON.

As a part of living, you will no doubt change your perspectives, views and priorities over time. This is why this work is evergreen, it is a practice that I invite you to embed into how you know yourself to be as a designer and consider revisiting from time to time.

MY VALUES SUMMARY.

THIS IS MY VALUES SUMMARY. I'VE GROUPED MY RESULTS IN THREE COLUMNS BASED ON THEIR IMPORTANCE, YOU MIGHT LIKE TO DO THE SAME.

MOST IMPORTANT

SELF-DIRECTION
Self-direction values are about thinking and acting independently. For people who value self-direction highly, it is very important to be free to choose their own goals and actions and to rely upon themselves. They want to learn and explore different topics and ways of thinking and to be original and creative.

UNIVERSALISM-NATURE
Universalism-nature values are about caring for the natural environment and for all animals. For people who value universalism-nature highly, it is critical to protect the environment from pollution and destruction. It is important for them to preserve the water, land, air, plants and animals for future generations.

UNIVERSALISM-SOCIETAL
Universalism-societal values are about wanting everyone to have equal opportunities in life. For people who value universalism-societal highly, the welfare of all the people in the world is very important. They want to understand and accept people who are different from themselves and to help people who have less than themselves.

BENEVOLENCE
Benevolence values are about caring for people you are close to, your family and friends. For people who value benevolence highly, it is very important to put the welfare of their family and friends ahead of their own. It is important for them to be helpful, responsible and dependable.

SECURITY

Security values are about being safe personally and living in a secure and stable society. For people who value security highly, it is very important to avoid any danger, risk or uncertainty. They want to live in a well-ordered, predictable environment. They want their society to be safe for their family and others, with a government that can protect them against threats.

ACHIEVEMENT

Achievement values are about seeking success according to social standards. For people who value achievement highly, it is very important to be ambitious, to achieve their goals and to show how capable and competent they are. They want to succeed in life and get ahead. They seek to influence and impress others and to be recognised for their success.

HEDONISM

Hedonism values are about seeking pleasure and enjoyment in life. For people who value hedonism highly, it is very important to enjoy life's pleasures, to have fun and indulge themselves. They want to relax, enjoy and pamper themselves.

CONFORMITY

Conformity values are about adhering to rules and to others' expectations. For people who value conformity highly, it is very important to follow rules and regulations and to meet all their obligations. They want to behave properly and to avoid upsetting others. They want to be polite and to avoid doing anything people would say is wrong.

TRADITION

Tradition values are about following cultural and religious traditions. For people who value tradition highly, it is very important to maintain, observe and respect the traditional practices, ideas and ways of thinking of their family, religion or ethnic group.

POWER

Power values are about seeking to control people and resources. For people who value power highly, it is very important to control others and to be wealthy. They want to have the authority or power to dominate others and get them to do what they want. Being rich and having high status is important to them.

STIMULATION

Stimulation values are about seeking new and exciting things to do. For people who value stimulation highly, it is very important to live an exciting life filled with variety and novelty. They enjoy change and adventure and like to try lots of new things. They tend to seek thrilling experiences.

LEAST IMPORTANT

To sum up

Our values drive and guide us and in turn the work we do. Our various values operate together in the background creating both potency, clarity and tension in what we prioritise and how we show up. Knowing our own values, and being able to understand other people's, is essential to knowing and harnessing our own unique design character.

The work of uncovering your own values sets up the practices you will leverage forever as a designer to become clearer and clearer about how you influence the direction and outcomes of your design work. Just by showing up.

Just by being you.

NEXT

Values shape how we see and respond to people and circumstances. Knowing where best to apply your attention and focus to achieve both meaningful outcomes and operate in alignment with your values is supportive of a satisfying design practice.

02

ATTENTION

We can only create what we pay attention to, that's why where you place your attention matters.

There are things you will naturally attend to, and things you will naturally ignore.

Knowing what you are likely to ignore will help you become a more inclusive designer.

WHAT GRABS YOUR ATTENTION HAS YOUR FOCUS.

02

We've established the fundamental roles values play in how you orient yourself in your life, and your work. In this chapter, we will explore attention and how it directs your energy.

Understanding this connection between your values and your attention is essential in helping you see things you may unconsciously overlook.

In this chapter we use scenarios taken from real-life design work to explore how your values translate into attention. This will create some realisations you can bring into your own work context.

Once we understand the places we are typically drawn towards, we can then deliberately direct our attention toward the places we are not naturally drawn. These places are gaps in our awareness.

Being able to do this makes you a more mindful and inclusive designer—one who is proficient at understanding your own biases and how to make room for new perspectives and insights.

An IMPORTANT CONSIDERATION

I was listening to The Master and His Emissary by Iain McGilchrist (McGilchrist, 2009) recently and I was taken aback by his comment:

"ATTENTION IS A MORAL ACT."

The sense I get from this statement is what we notice and give energy to, we privilege—we choose to hold as more important.

This choice perhaps, is not always a real choice. We are not necessarily aware of what we are NOT choosing, and for design and designers, this is an important consideration. This is why attention is important in design.

The act of design is to bring about change in the world, whether it is a small act or a grand one. Design is a process of creation and making, of bringing form to abstract ideas and thoughts. The choices we make about what goes out into the world, and what form it can take have inherent within them our biases, whether conscious or unconscious. *The more work we can do to better define our design character, the more resilient we will be to the unintended consequences of unconscious designing.*

As designers, we work with diverse populations with vastly different experiences to our own. To get as close to their experience of their reality as possible, we also need to look for insight in places we wouldn't naturally be drawn to. *We can only design from where our attention is.*

Attention and Energy

I tend to think of attention like a beam of sunlight; whatever you shine it on tends to grow, or animate, or become interesting. To keep moving with nature as a metaphor, I see values as a source of water for root systems. Plants will naturally grow towards water underground and towards sunlight above ground.

Values are what draws your attention, as a result of that attention you put energy into whatever your attention is captured by. This is why it is essential for us to be literate in our own values, and understand the link between them, our attention and where we are directing our energy.

To understand the importance of attention to our work, we first need to understand it a little better. And then we can talk about the link between attention and energy, and its relevance to design.

"ENERGY *flows where* ATTENTION *goes.*" Tony Robbins

Types of Attention

Attention is its own massive field in neuroscience, so big and dense it has its own gravitational field. Here, I'm going to focus on my own particular interest in attention and its relevance to the practice of design. If you'd like to learn more about others' views on attention, I've included some reading in the Resources.

I like to think of attention as current awareness. It is where your awareness is in the present moment, to the exclusion of other stimuli. Mostly, we can direct our attention (there's an exercise a little later that demonstrates this) and sometimes it gets captured or hijacked. Think about when you hear an unexpected sound, or someone from across the room expressing a strong emotion, or your notifications pop up with an email you've been waiting for. You move your attention. The more we are conscious of where our attention is resting, the more appropriately and deftly we are able to direct it or redirect it.

To influence where your attention is requires mastering a couple of skills:

This goes back to Chapter 1 where we learnt about how we tend to pay attention naturally to aspects of our work that are aligned with our value sets and tend to 'not see' or pay less attention to things we don't value.

Let's first understand the different types of attention we have.

SUSTAINED ATTENTION

Sustained Attention is our ability to focus on one task for an extended period of time.

This refers to our ability to focus on one thing for a continuous period, sometimes referred to as concentration or vigilance depending on the context that requires this type of attention. Sustained attention is what we use to be able to learn, to complete any sequence of tasks, to socialise, and to participate in many other human activities. It is a foundational ability that enables us to develop how we think and behave. It is useful to think of the three stages of sustained attention and the role they play in our work (DeGangi and Porges, 1990). The three stages are:

The 'Attention getting' part is the most important as this is the point at which we can intervene and direct our attention to where it will focus while we work.

1. ATTENTION GETTING

2. ATTENTION HOLDING

3. ATTENTION RELEASING

SELECTIVE ATTENTION

This is our ability to focus on a particular stimulus in our environment whilst deliberately ignoring all others. I tend to use the 'cocktail party' effect as an example of this. Although this is really something our auditory systems are facilitating, our ability to choose to listen to the person standing in front of us rather than the many other conversations that are occurring simultaneously, is an example of selective attention.

For example, imagine a scenario where you are designing with citizens from rural communities. You may be trying to understand their current experience of a general health service, and then working with them to improve effectiveness. If you happen to have 'Stimulation' as one of your core values, you may find you are naturally drawn toward ideas that are novel and technologically oriented. You may not give as much of your attention to ideas that are more about back-to-basics approaches. Knowing that this is your tendency, you can try to balance where you are directing your attention to bring balance to your work.

Selective Attention is our ability to choose what to notice and what to ignore.

DIVIDED ATTENTION

This is where science and lived experience seem to be at odds. While there are plenty of divided attention studies suggesting that we are not that great at performing two tasks simultaneously, we seem to think that's not true.

> *"I can talk to someone and wash the dishes at the same time."*
>
> *"I can speak with my friends, play a game and study for my Biology test, no problem."*

The truth is, when we look at it objectively/scientifically, there tends to be a performance cost with divided attention, especially if what we are focussing on is new to us. As we become practised at a task, we can learn to do multiple things at the same time (like driving a car), but change the nature of one of the tasks, like increase the trickiness of the traffic, or receive a text message, and we are back to reduced performance once more.

The notion of multi-tasking comes from the belief that attention is limitless. One thing we do know and probably experience daily is that certainly is not the case. Again, there are some links for you to follow in the

Divided Attention is our ability to attend to more than one thing simultaneously.

Resources section if you'd like to read about this in more depth.

Divided attention is also required when our work as designers is spread across multiple projects. Although this is not exactly the same thing, it does have a similar effect.

CONTEXT SWITCHING IS COSTLY.

It takes time to reconnect with the design context and where you're up to in the work, and then takes time again for you to start performing in that task. Just like divided attention, there's a performance cost. It is important for you to know when your attention is being divided across too many design jobs for you to perform at your best, so you can then have the appropriate conversations to advocate for your own practice.

MINDFUL ATTENTION

Now I don't know if mindful attention has earned its place among the other attention categories, but I think it is different enough, and relevant enough, to add it here. More researchers are choosing to blend the field of spiritual practice and neuro-imaging to understand the effects different mindfulness practices can bring about in the brain. Most relevant of these differences is the increased capacity to regulate your internal experience and ability to *remain in the moment* without launching into thoughts, analysis and meaning making (Desbordes, 2012).

Mindful attention is our ability to attend internally, to our breath and our body.

Often this is done through breath or body focus and this act alone has the immediate effect of bringing your focus to the current moment. This form of attention is open, receptive and processes stimulus without applying a meaning. As people, we tend to be pretty quick/eager to interpret what is happening in front of us. Whether a research data point, or an interaction across a crowded cafe, or what you think your dog might be feeling. Mindful attention is a superpower in the work of ethical, conscious design and an essential attribute in any design character development work.

MINDFUL ATTENTION IS WORTH CULTIVATING THE MOST.

Imagine...

A design scenario where you are in a group interview. Different people are sharing different aspects of their experience. They are just describing what happened and what they did. Something someone says provokes a thought within you that has you interpret and extrapolate the meaning behind what has just been said. That extrapolated meaning then results in an immediate idea for a solution. You feel the familiar warm glow in your chest as the life raft of an answer floats by to save you from the sea of ambiguity.

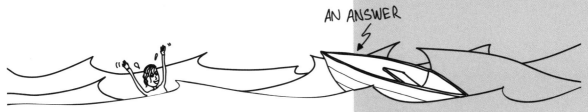

AN ANSWER

SEA OF AMBIGUITY

Mindful attention allows you to put the meaning making on hold, to bring your attention back to the present moment, and really focus on what is actually being said, as it is happening in front of you, with as little interpretive mind chatter as possible. This builds within you the ability to really listen and to be present with other human beings, giving you the most access to sharing their experience.

"No puedo caminar por los suburbios

en la soledad de la noche sin

pensar que la noche nos agrada

porque suprime los detalles ociosos,

tal como lo hace nuestra memoria."

Jorge Luis Borges

"I CANNOT WALK THROUGH THE SUBURBS

IN THE SOLITUDE OF THE NIGHT WITHOUT

THINKING THAT THE NIGHT PLEASES US

BECAUSE IT SUPPRESSES IDLE DETAILS,

JUST AS OUR MEMORY DOES."

Jorge Luis Borges

Types of Energy

REMEMBER THE QUOTE
FROM A FEW PAGES BACK?
LET'S TALK ABOUT THAT.

"Energy flows where attention goes." Tony Robbins.

Staying with the metaphor of attention being like a focussed sunbeam, we can understand why, when we attend to something, we expend energy toward it. When we conceive of our work as designers in this way, we can become quite discerning about where to direct our attention and so, our energy.

First let's define the word

ENERGY.

It is used a lot these days, in all sorts of contexts, so I really want to be clear here. I am not referring to the types of energy we were taught at school when we did science. I'm talking more about the type of energy we use when paying attention to certain things.

We will explore four types of energy, intellectual, emotional, relational and physical.

INTELLECTUAL

The energy that we most often expend as knowledge workers is intellectual energy, and we do that by *thinking.* The brain is about 2% of our body weight, but uses 20% of our energy, resting metabolic rate (RMR) to be more precise (Jabr, 2012). THAT'S A LOT. Since we are expending a lot of energy just by thinking, it's best we do it on productive thinking as much as possible. Now granted, for us un-enlightened folks, we can't necessarily control every single thought that passes through our minds, but we can learn to become aware of what we are thinking and then switch things up if those thoughts aren't particularly supportive of the task in front of us.

For example, think of a design critique session. You have put a lot of energy (of all types) into creating the concepts up for review. The critique session results in more work than you'd hoped, with more critical points raised than you expected. Hours after the session has concluded, you find yourself ruminating. Trying to understand why people did what they did, analysing whether it was something personal, trying to use all your design research superpowers to uncover the motivations of those present. Rather than using your intellectual energy on this detective work, it would be more productive directed toward the changes that need to be made.

BUILDING THE AWARENESS OF WHERE YOUR ENERGY IS BEING EXPENDED IS THE FIRST STEP TOWARDS INCREASING YOUR MASTERY AS A DESIGNER.

EMOTIONAL

You know when you read a book and you're left talking about it for weeks, months even, and those who are often with you have to withstand you talking about it ad nauseam? That's what happened when I read Power vs Force by David R. Hawkins (Hawkins, 2012). It affected me because his ground-breaking work measured the small shifts in a human body's electromagnetic field as it experienced different emotions.

We experience different energetic states as we feel different types of emotions. How is this relevant to design I hear you ask?

I have always maintained that design, especially that which uses participatory design methods, isn't just an intellectual pursuit; it requires a lot of your heart as well. Emotional literacy is critical to discerning what you are feeling as you make sense of the context within which you are designing and the cohort you are designing with (whether that's your team or those you are ultimately in service of). This takes energy, and we need to pay attention to how much energy we are expending on our own and others' emotions.

Sometimes it is necessary to sit with something that might be painful, or hilarious, and give it the time and energy it needs to communicate an insight. And sometimes, it is time to move on and start paying attention to something else. Awareness of the emotional energy you are expending in your work is essential to keeping you safe.

RELATIONAL

I pay a lot of attention to relational aspects of design and so this is where a lot of my energy flows. This is also because of my values, as you'll see from Chapter 1, I have strong universalism-societal and benevolence values. So naturally, this is where my attention likes to rest. *Relational energy is that which exists between things.* Whether it is between people, or between concepts or between journey steps. Understanding and paying attention to how things are related to each other is its own unique energy.

Remember, paying attention to the interconnectivity between those in your team, those you are designing with or in some circumstances on behalf of, and those who are overseeing the work, all have their own form of relational energy. Building your awareness of this form of energy, and directing your attention toward it, helps you deliberately design these relationships to be in best support of the people doing the work.

PHYSICAL

The form of energy we are the most familiar with. The energy we use when we are moving our bodies. Perhaps what we are not that familiar with is the self-awareness that is required to connect with your own body to check in and get curious about its current energetic state. *Your body and how it is feeling carries a lot of information about your work.* Whether it is during ideation, or facilitating a workshop, or reading through a draft report, our body is always talking to us. Becoming attuned to the signals that are present in your body provides you with greater access to your energetic and emotional state. Emotional and physical energy are very tightly coupled in this regard.

Paying attention to this form of energy, which is more aligned with mindful attention than the others, helps you access the practices you need to keep yourself fit and healthy to do the work. Often we don't pay attention to what our body feels like, so it is often neglected.

Establishing good practices to attend to and provide energy for your body is just as important as honing your intellectual skills.

STRONG DESIGN CHARACTER REQUIRES A STRONG BODY TO GO WITH IT.

How this is relevant to design

When we look at what's out there regarding attention and design, it is typically how to design for attention, rather than the role attention plays in directing design. We tend to forget that a human being is creating the designs, and

THE CHARACTER OF THE HUMAN BEING IS WHAT DIRECTS DESIGN DECISIONS.

Every chapter in this book provides another perspective on what informs the design decisions and judgements you make on a daily basis. This book has the sole purpose to create increased clarity within you about what motivates your design practice, why you gravitate towards certain types of design and then what to do with this knowledge.

Everything we cover in this book can be used as a framework or a heuristic to develop your own design character. Discussing attention and energy just after we've explored our values is to help bring heightened awareness to your work as a designer. *Most importantly, to ascertain whether you are paying the kind of attention to everything that requires it.*

When we think about the link between attention and energy, we see that attending to parts of our work that naturally draw our interest will be the most well formed and resolved, as they have received most of our energy. Understanding the values that are less motivating for you helps you direct your attention, and hence energy, toward those other aspects of your work. You can use your knowledge about different forms of energy as a checklist to see whether you are balanced in the approach you're taking with your work.

For example, you may ask yourself:

"Have I only given this work my intellectual attention? I seem to have a very well-formed analysis, with amazing functional requirements and a technical specification, but I can't really articulate how I want people to feel while using this service or product I'm creating."

This indicates some emotional energy is required to be expended, which suggests you need to pay attention to the emotive aspects of the work.

Alternatively, there may be something that isn't sitting right with you. You don't really know what it is, you can't put words to it yet, but you feel uncomfortable. ***This is your body speaking to you.*** Remember, we have more than one brain. Even though we like to think the grey matter in our skull is doing all the work, our heart, gut and body are also wired with nerves and neurones and 'think' in a different way to what we are used to. So, it is time to bring your attention inward to your body, slow down and listen to what it is trying to say.

These aspects all contribute to cultivating a mindful, ethical design practice with a strongly developed design character.

ATTENTION DIRECTION EXERCISE

The best way to become familiar with where your attention is resting is to play with it. The following exercises are designed to help you become familiar with the different forms and directions of attention.

01

Sit somewhere comfortable where you can cycle through these steps a few times.

02

Find something to focus on that is outside of you. It could be an object to look at, a flower or a tree, or a sound to lock on to. Once you've found it, notice how you move through the attention getting and attention holding phase. Hold your attention there for three minutes.

03

Stay with this attention, resting on this single object for three minutes without shifting your attention elsewhere.

THIS IS SELECTIVE ATTENTION, BEING ABLE TO CHOOSE ONE THING TO FOCUS ON WITHOUT BEING DISTRACTED.

THIS IS SUSTAINED ATTENTION. IF YOUR ATTENTION DRIFTS, BRING IT BACK TO THE ORIGINAL OBJECT.

Now move your attention from being focused on something outside of you, to something inside of you. You can bring that image of the object inside and see it in your mind's eye by closing your eyes. You can move your attention to your breath and stay with that for **five breaths**.

You might then move your attention to a part of your body that might be a bit sore or tight, and see what the body is telling you to do to address that sensation.

THIS IS MINFDUL ATTENTION.

Take some time to connect with the quality of each attention type and reflect on the following questions:

1. What was your experience of holding your attention externally for three minutes? Was it easy or difficult? Did your mind wander?

2. What did it feel like to move your attention from being externally oriented to internally oriented? Was it easy or difficult? Did it feel different? If so, in what way?

3. What lessons can you bring into your design practice?

NOTE

Step 5 is just as important as the other steps. This is the reflexive part of your practice. It is through this inquiry that you are able to integrate what you are learning in a way that actually makes a difference to how you design.

"*Whatever we put our* ATTENTION ON *will grow* STRONGER *in our life.*"

Maharishi Mahesh Yogi

THE LINK BETWEEN ATTENTION & VALUES

This exercise is to help you reflect on how your values direct your attention and how that manifests specifically in a design context.

01

Using your values summary from the first chapter, reflect on how your values may influence your perception and direct your attention in the project scenario below.

Remember, when your attention is drawn toward something, it is drawn away from something else.

The scenario: You have done a bunch of design research into how people engage with online financial services; in particular, mortgage applications. The data is in and you are working with a group to start the analysis and synthesis process. You have data ranging from task-related activities and emotional journeys, to interviews about customer motivations and aspirations.

02

Some questions to help you with your reflection:

1. Knowing my stronger values, what will my attention be naturally drawn towards?

2. Knowing my weaker values, what will I need to consciously pay attention to?

3. Having understood this, what will I do differently next time I'm in a similar design context?

To sum up

What we attend to, we direct energy towards.

The type of attention we give,
the flavour of energy we focus on,
has a direct impact on the outcomes
of our work as designers. Becoming
adept at being aware of what is drawing
your attention, and to observe whether
that focus best serves you and the
job at hand, is a practice that reaps
long-term rewards.

NEXT

We take a
short trip down
Philosophy Lane
and understand a
little more about
ethics, the role ethics
plays in design and
designing, and how
it intersects and
merges with
your values.

03

ETHICS

Whether you know it or not,
as a designer, your actions
result in shared realities.
These realities are comprised
of services, systems, policies,
products, places, businesses
and interactions.

The experiences of these then
shape who we are as people.
It affects how we are in the
world and our view of it.
Being a designer with a clear
sense of ethics has never
been more important.

WE CANNOT TALK ABOUT DESIGN CHARACTER WITHOUT DISCUSSING ETHICS.

The intention of this book is not to describe what your design character should be. It is to support the work that must be done to discover that for yourself.

Think of this book, like a guided encounter with your own design character. Ethics establish the framework that has your moral code embedded in it.

This framework leans on your values and your principles, and it helps guide your action towards something aligned and authentic to you. It feeds how you communicate, the boundaries you establish, what you say yes to and what you say no to. All of these things are happening right now in your work, perhaps unconsciously. In this chapter, you will understand what ethics are, the role ethics plays in design and why it is important for you to do the work to create your own framework to inform how you design.

What are ethics?

Philosophy is a fascination of mine, not a competency. The first philosophy book I read was called This is Not a Book by Michael Picard, the contents of which still creep into my mind today. It is a great summary of 'popular philosophy' and it seems, like me, Michael also believes in experiments to help integrate knowledge. Throughout the book there are puzzles and thought experiments that have your neurons tied up in knots. You can't really walk away from this book without an insight into the simultaneous inconsistency and directive power of our beliefs and world view.

Ethics, one of the main branches of philosophy, is concerned with how to decide on the best action. As humans, we are different from other species in that we can conceive of many alternatives for action. These actions can be in direct opposition to our instincts, and form no meaningful contribution to our survival (in fact this is often the case!).

Ethics is the field that introduces critical reflection to how we live our lives. In fact, while on a Design Ethics panel I remember asking the ethicist, "What is an ethical life?", and I remember his response,

"AN ETHICAL LIFE IS AN EXAMINED ONE."

In fact, Socrates went so far as to say, *"An unexamined life is not worth living."*

"DESIGN *can only succeed if guided by an* ETHICAL VIEW."

John Vassos

I like the simplicity of this answer and I also like that it is devoid of judgement and projection. He didn't say living an ethical life means you look after your neighbour and be kind to the planet. There are of course clear differences between ultimate good and evil and we perhaps need to believe that as a species we do have a collective sense of what is good and right for society. How we situate ourselves firstly within that, and specifically as designers, is the purpose of this work.

There is a beautiful summary of ethics in Beard and Longstaff (2018) and they propose a great framework that is a solid example of an ethical framework. Their focus is around technology but still resonates with the same principles we need to apply when designing.

"The designers and developers of technology should accept responsibility for their design decisions—including the technical means by which artefacts bring ethical principles to life. For us to specify a set of 'rules' would be to diminish this sense of responsibility, it risks creating a culture of compliance rather than a culture of genuine responsibility.'
Beard and Longstaff (2018)

Types of ethics

To help guide your thinking about your own ethical principles, we'll first need to understand the different types of ethics that exist. You will probably resonate more with some than others, but all need to be present when considering your own framework.

THE FOLLOWING IS A SUMMARY OF THE DIFFERENT THEORIES OF ETHICS.

BENTHAM

CONSEQUENTIALISM

Good outcomes—achieving good outcomes is the focus.

In consequentialism, you are concerned about the outcome your actions will take and will guide them so they result in something you perceive as positive rather than negative. Remember, values play a key role in perceiving what is good, they set your standards. So if you have strong benevolence values, your ethics might direct action that is good for others; or if you have hedonism as a strong value, a 'good' outcome might be a personal pleasure being fulfilled.

KANT

ARISTOTLE

DEONTOLOGY

Fulfilling obligations—dutiful action is the focus.

This theory of ethics seems to sit in opposition to consequentialism, in that it says we need to fulfil our duties, to do what is right, regardless of the outcome. This theory believes that all humans have intrinsic value and must be treated in line with that value at all costs, with no compromises. A pure deontologist would not sacrifice a single human life to save one million, because the act of killing someone is morally wrong.

TELEOLOGY

Achieving purpose—clarity of ultimate purpose is the focus.

This theory believes we cannot make a correct moral judgment if we are unclear of its ultimate purpose. Teleology insists that we make decisions that are in line with their ultimate reason for being. We need to be clear about the purpose of what we create, the activities we engage in and the organisation and communities we are a part of. If we are clear about the ultimate purpose of our lives, our actions should be aligned with that purpose.

SOCRATES

ROUSSEAU

VIRTUE

Virtuous action—cultivating good character is the focus.

This theory believes our actions shape our character and the more we do a certain action, the more likely we are to repeat it. These actions can either be good and virtuous, or bad and vicious (virtues and vices).

There is a practicality that is present in this theory. It is less black and white than Deontology. There is an understanding these virtuous actions exist on a continuum, and that a virtuous person makes clear choices as they learn to discern what is right and good for themselves.

CONTRACTUALISM

Retaining trust and legitimacy— consent and fair exchange is the focus.

This theory, also known as social contract theory, relies on the consent given when entering into an agreement for the exchange of value and power. Adherents believe as long as there is consent for the exchange of power versus freedom for example, and the rights and responsibilities of those involved are clear and agreed, the actions that occur within this agreement are legitimate. This theory defines how governments retain legitimacy, only through citizens trusting the social contract and granting it authority to do so.

SARTE

EXISTENTIALISM

Taking responsibility—radical freedom and responsibility is the focus.

This theory believes that human beings are 'radically free' to act as we wish and are able to shape who we will become. This radical freedom also comes with responsibility. To act with freedom also means to take responsibility for those actions. This way of living, to be wholly responsible for the shape of our lives and our personhood, can feel overwhelming and difficult. To cope with this, we often outsource decisions, from what we should have for dinner, to the person we ought to be, but that comes at a cost. To existentialists, it can feel like a betrayal internally, like an act of bad faith to oneself, because you are not enacting the freedom you ultimately believe you have.

TO LIVE AN ETHICAL LIFE WE NEED TO LIVE A REFLECTIVE ONE.

With this embryonic understanding of the field of ethics you now have access to a little more structure for your reflections on how you act and enact your values. The next step is to understand how ethics fits into the world of design so you can get busy creating your own ethical framework.

AN IMPORTANT NOTE

The ethical theories presented on the previous pages are all informed by the Western (and masculine) perspective. This is the society into which I have been socialised. There are many different traditions of thought (Indigenous, Eastern, Africana, Feminist for example) that have different perspectives of ethics. To provide just one example, the statement below highlights the difference in perspectives between Feminist Theories of Ethics and the ones I have listed previously:

> *"Traditional ethics prizes masculine cultural traits like 'independence, autonomy, intellect, will, wariness, hierarchy, domination, culture, transcendence, product, asceticism, war, and death,' and gives less weight to culturally feminine traits like 'interdependence, community, connection, sharing, emotion, body, trust, absence of hierarchy, nature, immanence, process, joy, peace, and life'."* Feminist Ethics (2022)

Anyone who is interested in creating an ethical framework that is holistic and incorporates broader perspectives should become familiar with other forms of Ethical Theory.

This realisation struck me hard as I was researching and writing this chapter. This is a huge field far outside my current area of expertise so I don't feel equipped to do it justice here... yet. So instead, I will create a big bright neon sign that says, 'look here' so you can do your own research and become informed as well. In the Resources section, I've shared the texts that I have started to read to build my understanding to help inform my own practice.

LOOK HERE

DESIGN JUSTICE
FEMINIST ETHICS
CULTURES OF CARE

"*This is my*
SIMPLE RELIGION.

There is no need for temples;
        no need for complicated philosophy.
Our own brain, our own heart is our temple;
        philosophy is kindness."

Dalai Lama

Why we need to talk about ethics

By now we have a sense of what ethics are and the questions they ask of us. The main reason why we need to talk about ethics in the context of design is because the very common question, "Which concept shall we prioritise and progress to the next stage" is actually an ethical one. Design is the process of bringing things into form, whether it is abstract or concrete. These forms engage with us through the 'social scripts' they embody. Leyla Acaroglu in her article The Silent Social Scripter refers to the reciprocal, or ontological, power of design.

WHAT WE DESIGN AND PUT OUT INTO THE WORLD THEN INFLUENCES AND DESIGNS US IN RETURN.

By saying 'designs us in return' I refer to how what we create directly influences our behaviour and interactions (like smartphones).

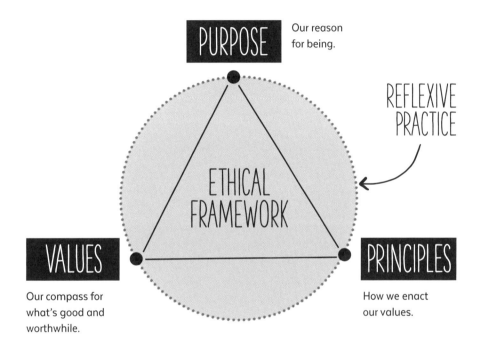

PURPOSE — Our reason for being.

REFLEXIVE PRACTICE

ETHICAL FRAMEWORK

VALUES — Our compass for what's good and worthwhile.

PRINCIPLES — How we enact our values.

FIGURE 3.1
Incorporating an ethical framework into your design practice.

The built environments we create initiate certain experiences and activate interactions. The mechanisms we use provide access to information and knowledge that then influence how we perceive, and exist, in that world. ***The only way to avoid ethics in our decision making as designers is to avoid making a conscious decision, ever.***

To support your journey in incorporating an ethical framework into your design practice, we'll build on the work we've already done with our values. There is a neat way we can think about ethics that guides our work in defining our frame for designing. You'll probably see three of the theories of ethics are represented in the framework above already, it is great place to start.

PURPOSE

One of the first things we cover in the Deep Leadership work I do is Purpose. It is difficult, and most people don't spend a lot of time considering this question. You may know someone who has a very clear sense of purpose and is working every day to be in alignment with that, and you may know more people who don't really feel they have one or need one. I have worked with leaders who fall into both camps and every other camp in between. I have come to realise you don't need to have a purpose to be successful in life *but I think you do need to have a purpose if you want to 'live on purpose'*.

Living on purpose brings us back to ethics—to know whether you are or not requires you to reflect and examine your life and work.

In the context of design, it is essential to have a clear sense of purpose of what you are working on, and to what ultimate outcome. It gives you an unmoving target that provides the overarching context for your work, informing decisions to progress work and an aligning force keeping things on track. Designing without a sense of purpose for your work is like designing in the dark. I have noticed that the word 'purpose' in the context of design can be eye-roll inducing. "I don't care about the purpose of the work, this is a loyalty program, I just need the webpage updated now."

The purpose doesn't need to be epic and grand. In fact the best purpose is one that is clear, simple and concise. "We are updating the webpage so our customers have better engagement/improved user experience and ultimately choose to stay with us" is the ultimate reason for being for that particular project. It reminds us why we are doing the work and is present as we design what customers will experience as a result of our work.

PURPOSE IS THE OVERARCHING 'WHY'. IT IS OUR CONTEXT FOR ACTION.

VALUES

These should be very familiar to you by now, so I won't spend too much time on them here. The relationship between values and purpose is the difference between context and judgment. Purpose explains why, values define what's good and worthwhile (according to you). You pay more attention to things you believe are worthwhile, and you are more likely to create more things in the world that you think are good. So it is worth spending time understanding and updating what those values are and how they ought to influence your work.

VALUES SHOW US WHAT'S GOOD AND WORTHWHILE.

PRINCIPLES

The principles are the way in which your values are enacted within the context of your purpose. See how it all fits together nicely? On a recent walk with my dog Charlie, I was contemplating the difference between how people express their values.

We may find ourselves on opposing ends of a political argument but actually share the same value. The value of benevolence could be expressed quite differently depending on the principles that informed your action. For example, you may express benevolence by taking care of people less fortunate than yourself, or you choose to do the same for people just like yourself. We can see how, although our values may be shared, the way they are enacted in the world can be different.

PRINCIPLES GUIDE OUR ACTIONS.

"With ALL architects CARING should be a

MORAL *imperative."*

E. Fay Jones

HOW TO CREATE YOUR OWN ETHICAL FRAMEWORK.

Don't set yourself the task of getting it all sorted in one sitting. This is a work in progress. This exercise (as with many in this book) is designed to be returned to over and over again. Take your time with it, remember much of the material in here is slow work. It is contemplative, reflective and deep.

01

READ

Using the resources at the back of this book as a starting point, do some reading into other examples of ethical frameworks. The list we have curated ranges from Indigenous design principles to ethical tech frameworks.

02

CONNECT WITH PURPOSE

To create an achievable scope, start with a recent project you've been working on. Using the Purpose, Values, Principles framework ask yourself the following question:

1. What was the reason for being for this project? Try to think of this from an outcome perspective. What was the project ultimately in service of?

03

CONNECT WITH YOUR VALUES

Connect back with your values and look at the alignment between the work and your value system.

1. Where is there alignment between your project, it's purpose and values with your own?
2. Where is there dissonance?

CREATE SOME PRINCIPLES

Using this reflection around your values in the context of the purpose of your work, start to list out some principles that you believe will guide ethical action the next time you do a project like this. Leverage the work that has come before to guide your thinking into what these principles might be.

Some examples from my own practice:

1. Always seek engagement from those directly affected by your work.
2. Understand and share power appropriately.
3. Communicate often with transparency of decision making.
4. Be clear about your intentions, values and express your boundaries.
5. Participate in establishing safety for all involved.
6. Maximise positive outcomes, minimise bad—our shared future is a stakeholder.
7. Design in inclusivity—no edge cases.

REPEAT FOR A FEW OTHER PROJECTS

We are intentionally starting in the detail so the thinking isn't too abstract and the principles are not too broad sweeping. We want to be clear about the principles so they can deliberately guide our action next time. Repeat the above process for a few other projects and see what patterns emerge.

NOTE

There is a section in *this human* book on page 131 (Purpose and Intention) that can help clarify Purpose and support your thinking in this exercise.

EXTRACT THE THEMES AND PATTERNS.

Have a look through the different principles you have written for the different projects and see if there are similarities emerging. You can then begin to abstract these principles to start forming ethical principles for your practice.

"*Design is paradoxical in many ways. It is simultaneously a*

PROCESS
and an OUTCOME.

A NOUN
and a VERB.

It is complete ENGAGEMENT
and NON ATTACHMENT.

It is COLLABORATION *and* SOLITUDE.

It is EMERGENCE *and* PERMANENCE.

Design is something we can CONTROL *and it is* UNCONTROLLABLE."

Nelson and Stolterman

What happens without ethics?

ETHICS *are the* ANTIDOTE *to* UNCONSCIOUS DESIGNING

It is because of the tensions and paradoxes mentioned on the previous page that I believe unconscious design is the most dangerous. It is participating in a world-creating process without being present to the creation as a human being. It is absolving responsibility for that design to someone else, the client, the boss, the team and it is not taking responsibility for your part in its creation. The best we can do in design is to know who is doing the designing (know who you are) and to be intentional about how we go about it.

ETHICS *bring* PRESENCE *to* YOUR WORK

Ethics provide a reflective frame that enables you to bring your presence to your work. Ethics are often associated with 'good'. Good is a troublesome word for me because its perception can be varied among people. The most important aspect of having an ethical framework to guide your work is that it enables *you to be present* when making design decisions, enabling you to make them contextually, deliberately and importantly, consciously.

ETHICS *provide a* SAFETY NET *for* ACCIDENTAL NEGATIVE OUTCOMES

Later in the book we will discuss power. An accidental negative impact might be that you conduct work with a group of people with a history of exploitation by those in power. If you do not understand the power you hold in the room, you may unconsciously participate in perpetuating the dynamic this group has experienced in the past. Even though it is far from your intention and world view. Doing the work in this book helps you understand who you are, and what you represent in the process of designing and brings awareness to ways you can mitigate these accidental negative outcomes.

It is also not possible to design only for positive outcomes. Even though that might be our intention.

NEW DESIGNS ALWAYS BRING SHADOWS WITH THEM.

This is part of the paradox of design, it is controllable and uncontrollable. When you release a design into the wild, it is difficult to predict what will happen to it.

The act of designing is to bring about change, which usually means that the previous version becomes obsolete or is replaced. Designs meet the needs of some more completely than others. They can provide near-term gain with long-term pain. Most of this can be minimised by bringing awareness and ethics to your practice while at the same time accepting that design's very nature is paradoxical.

"To think dispassionately about what we design and why, as well as what the eventual consequences of our design intervention may be, is the basis of ethical thinking."

Victor Papenek

ACCEPTANCE IN DESIGN

This is a deep reflection exercise. We are in the most philosophical chapter, so this exercise is intended to facilitate some deep reflection into your acceptance of what design really is. This exercise is an acceptance practice.

01 BUILD FAMILIARITY

Become familiar with the following list of attributes of design:

Design is challenging: there are no right answers, there are no givens, it is not comprehensive.

Design is powerful: the act of design creates the world.

Design requires personal responsibility: designers are in service of others.

Design requires personal accountability: what we design, designs us and the outcome matters.

Design is paradoxical: it works with plurality, seemingly oppositional perspectives can co-exist.

Design requires disciplined character: the design cannot be separated from the designer.

Design has immense potential: it can ensoul, protect the ethical and just, create beauty, change human evolution.

02 REFLECT AND RECORD

Think critically about each statement in the list, ask yourself the following questions:

1. What happens inside you when you read the statements? How does it make you feel? Why?
2. Where do you feel resistance?
3. Where do you feel alignment?
4. What would you change?

03 INTEGRATE AND INCORPORATE

1. What realisations have bubbled to the surface you can act upon?
2. Could it be a different way you position design within your organisation, or within your own practice?
3. Will it change the way you relate to the act of designing, or how you teach design?
4. What are the implications of these realisations on you and your personal practice?

NOTE

On Page 189 in Nelson and Stolterman (2012), the authors list attributes of design that, in my view, we need to accept to fully step into our roles as responsible, ethical designers.

To sum up

Ethics guide our design judgements and actions in a direction that minimises accidental negative outcomes of our work. It ensures we are present in the varied design contexts in which we find ourselves and ensures our design action is considerate of those involved. It helps us remain aware and present while engaging in the act of design.

Design is inherently uncertain and we often make design judgements with incomplete information, that is its emergent nature. Strong sense of purpose for the work, clear connection with your values and established ethical principles create strong scaffolding for you to do meaningful and impactful work in the world.

NEXT

Next we will step outside of our inner selves (phew!) and understand the role of communication and self-care in your role as a designer. Understanding the interaction between these elements helps you enact your ethics in the context of your design work.

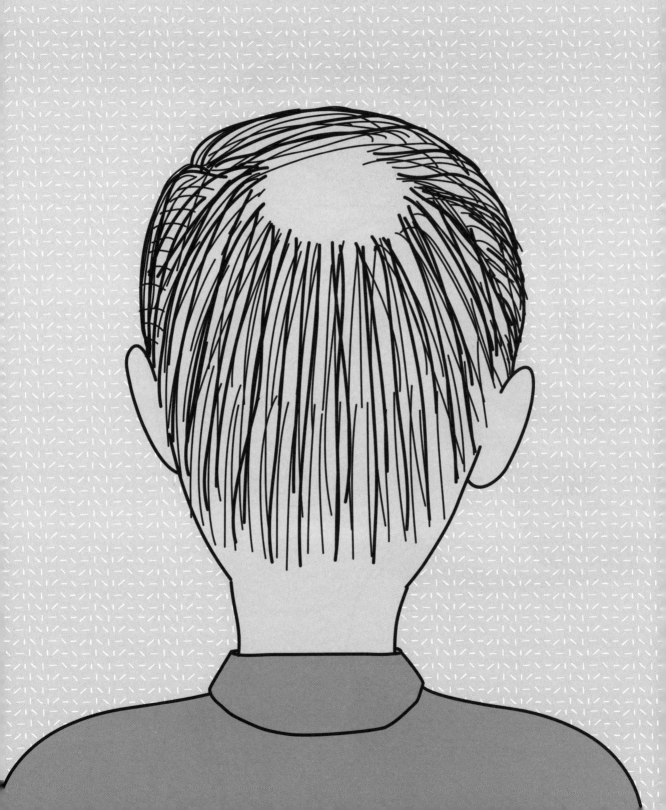

04

COMMUNICATION
& SELF-CARE

When we get clear about who we are and what we stand for, we develop the confidence and courage to speak up.

You may also experience resistance towards what you believe in, so it is critical to develop the communication skills to navigate difficult conversations.

With challenge and resistance comes the necessity for *self-care* so you can continue to do the great work the world needs.

04

In this chapter we learn about diverse ways to tackle difficult scenarios when ethics and values are challenged.

One of the by-products of knowing who you are as a designer is clarity about what you do and why.

THIS CLARITY BREEDS CONFIDENCE, AND CONFIDENCE ENERGISES COMMUNICATION.

We explore different scenarios and exercises that help you practise how to protect your values while still remaining collaborative and open. We also acknowledge the toll this awareness can take when working in challenging contexts and how to ensure you have the best self-care practices in place to support you and help you remain healthy and strong.

What clarity & confidence provide

I remember a comment by a past student,

> *"The stuff we work through is quite obvious really, when you think about it... [substantial pause and reflection]... but we don't really think about it, until you ask us to."*

This is a beautiful way to capture the nature of this work. **The questions are obvious and simple, but to consider them can be difficult.**

One of the gifts this work gives is the internal clarity and centredness you will feel about how you work that transforms into a deep confidence. This comes from knowing you have actually done the inner exploration, you have delved into the depths of your soul and have uncovered the bedrock you stand on. This clarity then creates a different tone in the way you talk about your work, and also the way people listen and respond to you. This is what I mean when I use the word 'potency'.

WITH CONFIDENCE AND CLARITY CAN COME CONFLICT.

Although mostly unavoidable in the world of effective design, we do our utmost to ensure conflict is the exception rather than the rule.

You will find it increasingly difficult to stay quiet when you think something is heading in a direction that doesn't sit well with you. You will find words start flowing from your mouth when otherwise they wouldn't, and most of the time it will feel pretty good.

Of course, as with any situation involving change, some will not like what you have to say. It may represent a slow down, a complication, or a 'back to the drawing board' scenario, which feels like it hampers their ability to proceed. They may also have a differing opinion and the clash makes them feel like they are being threatened. It's at these moments when frustration can creep in.

Before we get into how to deal with these situations, let's unpack what a difficult conversation actually is.

"NOTHING *will work unless* YOU DO."

Maya Angelou

THE ANATOMY *of a* DIFFICULT CONVERSATION

In 2014 I bought a book called Conscious Business—How to Build Value Through Values by Fred Kofman. There is much gold to be found in this book, relevant to us right now is how Kofman breaks down a difficult conversation. He says there are three elements:

1. THE 'IT'

The task that needs to happen. This is the impersonal, objective content of the conversation.

2. THE 'RELATIONSHIP'

The interpersonal dynamic, the nature of the relationship and its health.

3. THE 'SELF'

The personal dynamic, the inner dialogue, identity and self-esteem.

TO FURTHER ILLUSTRATE THIS, I'LL USE A SCENARIO TO HELP US
UNPACK IT. CHARLIE IS A SENIOR DESIGNER, AND BILLY IS A PROJECT MANAGER.

> "*Every kind of* PEACEFUL CO-OPERATION *amongst people is primarily built on* MUTUAL TRUST."
>
> *Albert Einstein*

The conversation between Charlie and Billy is a common one in design. The sense of frustration felt by both sides can make this conversation ***feel difficult.***

Let's have a look at what is happening here and the difference between what is said and what is being thought or felt.

Charlie is coming to this conversation already full. She has been working up to bringing this to her boss and is disappointed when Billy can only give her 15 minutes.

Billy is under pressure from many directions and has promised something to the client and is focussed on making that happen. To Billy, Charlie seems like a purist who is going to slow down the process. To Charlie, Billy doesn't understand design and can't create the conditions for her to do great work. Both are 'right'.

The 'it' part of this conversation is about the misuse of 'co-design' as a method within the project. Billy isn't familiar enough with design to know the difference so doesn't really care, and Charlie practices participatory design and believes collaboration and co-creation are the best ways to progress design effectively. She knows what they are doing IS NOT co-design, so it doesn't feel right to her to keep calling it that.

The 'relationship' part of this conversation is the dynamic between Billy and Charlie and their emotional connection. Because Billy hasn't given Charlie the time, she thinks Billy doesn't value her opinion.

To Billy, Charlie is showing a lack of understanding of the pressure they are under because they assume what Charlie is saying is going to have a negative impact on the deadline.

Charlie questions Billy's motives for misusing the term and Billy questions Charlie's business nous.

TRUST IS AT STAKE.

The 'self' part of this conversation relates to the inner questions and thoughts they are both experiencing that aren't being shared. Charlie is worried if she keeps talking she's going to fall out of favour with her boss, so she hesitates.

Billy is worried Charlie doesn't care if the project runs late. Both are feeling misunderstood. Billy may also be suppressing feelings of inadequacy because they don't understand the issue, and Charlie is worried about how she is coming across.

"A difficult conversation is difficult because we feel threatened in the three aspects of task, relationship and self."

Fred Kofman

Our automatic reaction is defensive and that brings out the worst in us. We are certain we know what is really happening and what needs to happen. Our certainty, however is false.

As a designer, you would be familiar with the feeling of keeping an open mind and listening with empathy to another. We often forget to do this when we are in work scenarios like the one above. How would this conversation have gone differently if Charlie saw Billy as a research participant instead of her boss?

This was exactly the approach I employed when I was working in a large organisation with a very early understanding of the role of design in business.

By listening to understand their reasoning, and getting curious about the context they worked in, and the pressures they felt, it helped me understand how to better advocate for the approaches and ideas I had.

LET'S ASSUME CHARLIE JUST FINISHED READING THIS BOOK AND ENGAGES IN THE SAME CONVERSATION WITH BILLY. NOTICE THE DIFFERENCE CLARITY BRINGS.

Great! I'll set it up.

As you can see, Charlie seems much more confident in this conversation. I dare say she seems quite a bit calmer as well in her thoughts.

Knowing this wasn't about design and was about her values being challenged helped Charlie get right to the core of what she wanted to discuss. When this happens, people tend to listen.

Billy sensed this was an important point Charlie was raising, and as the project manager, felt she needed to take this seriously. It can't be easily dismissed as 'designer purism' with the process, because Charlie has made it clear it is about her values. And the only way she can know this is because she has done the inner work.

"Unlike cynicism, hopefulness is hard-earned, makes demands upon us, and can often feel like the most indefensible and lonely place on Earth. Hopefulness is not a neutral position either. It is adversarial. It is the warrior emotion that can lay waste to cynicism.

*Each redemptive or loving act,
as small as you like... keeps the
devil down in the hole. It says the
world and its inhabitants have
value and are worth defending.
It says the world is worth
believing in. In time, we come
to find that it is so."*

Love, Nick Cave

HOW TO HAVE BETTER DIFFICULT CONVERSATIONS

Useful frameworks can be found in Chapter 3 (pages 79–105) in my first book, *this human,* that provide guidance on how to listen and how to give feedback. Later in that book, there is also a whole chapter on Connection (pages 107–123).

In this book, I want to talk about what you can develop within yourself to have more effective conversations in design.

01
USE ASSUMPTIONS FOR GOOD, NOT EVIL

For conversations to be effective, we must assume there is information we don't have and things to learn. We can create assumptions to help us in conversation as readily as we create assumptions that hinder us.

For example, you might assume the person is holding back information to protect you from further complexity or you may assume they are doing this to inhibit your progress. As you will see in the next point, you want to put yourself in the best position to have an effective, confident conversation rather than 'be right' about your assumptions. So work on getting yourself in the right space to do that.

02
SOLIDARITY OVER SELF-RIGHTEOUSNESS

Co-operation comes from solidarity rather than being right. Recognise what binds you rather than divides you.

Spend time preparing in this way before the conversation, so the energy you bring stems from a collegiate place rather than an adversarial one.

Commit to finding common ground rather than being validated and right.

EXPLORATION OVER DEFENSIVENESS

Use all you know about design and design research to help you through these conversations. Every conversation you have will most likely be with another human being. Even the most accomplished, senior person can feel unsure, vulnerable and inadequate.

We all have struggles and we all have insecurities. Remain curious and explore what is driving the other person in the direction they are heading, connect with their experience and gain insight into their position before trying to establish yours.

HEART FIRST, THEN HEAD

Before we can start talking about the content of the conversation, the 'it' part, the emotions need to be addressed. I don't mean this literally or explicitly. What I mean is to acknowledge the other person has emotion and charge around the issue just as you do, but for different reasons. This emotion needs to first be addressed before jumping into solution mode.

It can be addressed in a very simple statement that might be, "So I can understand your perspective better, can you tell me what's concerning you about this and why?" This signals to the other person you actually care, that you are approaching this with compassion.

'AND' OVER 'OR'

As a designer, you know there is always room for possibility and hope in every conversation.

Hence the Nick Cave quote on the previous pages.

To work towards a solution that incorporates two opposing perspectives takes commitment and creativity from both sides. For this to be available, all these factors need to be addressed.

Bringing this stance to any conversation in the vicinity of the design work you are doing increases the chances of the work being unique, well resolved and impactful.

Care of Self

As I embark on this section of this chapter, I find myself needing to share a little about my personal journey with self-care. It will give you context as to why I believe it is so critical and so vital to look after yourself, in order to perform well as a designer, and within life.

A few years ago, I was struggling with my energy levels and there were a few complicated health challenges popping up. I had been pushing pretty hard for many years, trying to ensure I was turning up in all aspects of my life in high definition. I slowly realised without downtime, without a deliberate practice around self-care (beyond what I was already doing with my morning meditation practice) I was in a cycle with diminishing returns.

This is when I started to ask myself why I put so much pressure on myself and what it was all in aid of. I guess the detail of that journey is for another day, but during this exploration I uncovered a few things I'd like to talk about in this section.

SELF-CARE IS NOT SELFISH.

Namely, our Western cultural understanding of the word 'productive' and the associated judgements that come with 'self-care'. These topics need to be addressed first before we can fully explore what self-care looks like in the context of this work.

PRODUCTIVITY *and* 'GRIND CULTURE'

We are indoctrinated and socialised into a culture of work of the 'daily grind'. There is almost an expectation 'work' is not something you will enjoy, it is positioned as a necessary toil and if we want to survive, we all have to learn how to do it.

If you want to do more than survive, then success means you work hard, give it your all and reach the targets you set for yourself or others set for you—to work hard for your money.

My point is subtle. I do believe in working hard, I do. I believe sometimes we need to push ourselves out of our comfort zones to grow and to experience the new and to learn. I also think the way we do this is critical.

The human body is fuelled by energy. It expends energy just by thinking and expends more by working. If there isn't the reverse cycle also in place, where you are replenished of energy, it isn't a sustainable equation.

If we choose to work hard, we also need to rest hard. ***We need to be hard at rest.*** I know it sounds odd, right? We also have an unhealthy relationship with resting. My biggest challenge was to readjust my relationship with rest. I felt guilty when I rested. I felt like I wasn't being productive and while I was snoozing on the couch for an hour, that meant something wasn't getting done for an hour. I have now understood resting is very productive.

WE HAVE AN UNDERSTANDING THAT OUR VALUE IS CONNECTED WITH OUR PRODUCTIVITY.

This is another by-product of the grind culture of work. This is particularly troublesome in the creative industries because creativity doesn't tend to work like that. I don't know about your experience with creativity, but I certainly experience it as evasive. Sometimes it shows up when I need it to, and sometimes it's on vacation drinking Pina Coladas under a coconut palm somewhere far far away.

We can't be productive all the time, and when we rest, we increase our chances of being productive. This of course looks very different for each of us.

WHY SELF-CARE
is SO IMPORTANT
to this WORK

We've covered this point a few times, I know. I don't mean to sound repetitive.

AS YOU GAIN CLARITY IN WHO YOU ARE AS A DESIGNER, YOU'RE ALSO GOING TO CREATE MORE CHANGE AROUND YOU.

This might take the form of sharpening the way you practice design, introducing new approaches, methods and tools into your team, or it might take the form of how you speak about the work you do and why you do it in that way. People are going to reach out to you more for clarity, because you have it, and demands on your time will increase. This is the natural result of you evolving your mastery as a designer. With this increased demand will come an increased need for you to meet those demands in efficient and effective ways. This of course includes knowing what to say yes to and more importantly (and more difficult) saying no to certain requests.

In addition to the increase in demand, your words will carry more weight. Clarity and confidence has that effect. So with more weight comes the increased likelihood people will listen and respond accordingly, creating change. Change takes energy and this is always in addition to the work you are doing, the change itself surrounds and infuses your work, but it also needs its own care and attention. To operate at this level, you'll need to change your practices around how to take care of yourself through this process.

"The difference between an amateur and a professional is in their habits. An amateur has amateur habits. A professional has professional habits. We can never free ourselves of habit. But we can replace bad habits with good ones."

Steven Pressfield

My self-care practice

After this experience, I needed to change the way I worked. I found that by doing the following things, I was reenergised, I was able to achieve more and I felt like I was doing less. I did the following:

I CHANGED MY RELATIONSHIP WITH TIME.

I realised my relationship with time was the wrong way around for me. It was in control of my schedule rather than my wellbeing and aspiration. I realised I was prioritising other people's needs for time with me. I started prioritising my own needs for time, which was difficult at first. But then I noticed my productivity increased, the world kept turning, and people didn't spontaneously combust because I couldn't meet with them right when they needed me to.

My relationship with time is more friendly now. I also have a new belief around time, that it is stretchy, not fixed. I'm sure there are some physicists out there who may be able to argue each way. I look forward to that conversation. But for now, this belief about the stretchiness of time helps me.

I know that what gets done during certain time intervals changes, it is completely different from day to day and it is directly proportional to how rested and healthy I feel. That understanding puts my attention on the right part of the equation. Rather than playing Tetris with my calendar, I focus on my body, mind and spirit.

I PRIORITIZED RESTING.

I reframed rest as a productive task. I now have rest scheduled in my calendar throughout the day. I rest after lunch, to give my body time to take a breather. I lie on a couch, hopefully in a patch of sun somewhere, and just close my eyes. I don't sleep because that doesn't feel good to me for the rest of the day. But I focus on how my body is feeling, perhaps I do a body scan, or I put on a guided meditation. I do this for 45 minutes, most days. For me, it feels like I add two stretchy time hours' worth of productivity by doing this.

I DOUBLED DOWN ON MIND AND BODYFULNESS.

I have an established reflective practice since 2006, when I started journalling about being pregnant with my son. It's a morning ritual that involves, sitting outside, with a cup of tea, and letting the words flow.

I added movement to this practice to help move my body before I started the day. This was not running, or anything strenuous. It was moving my body the way it wanted to move, not forcing it into any yoga pose, or time frame, or cardiac target. It was more about mindfulness than it was about exercise. This is something I continue to this day. It is a beautiful thing to honour your body in this way.

I BROKE RULES AROUND WORK.

We don't realise the rules we accept around what 'work' is and 'should be'. I have always had a tenuous relationship with rules anyway, so this felt more fun than difficult.

I broke the rule around 9am to 5pm and also about 'how much work' needed to be accomplished in each day. I did things in a way that wasn't a fixed routine, which is something that is restful for me. I know others would find that rather stressful.

The point was I was finding a cadence that worked with my energy levels. I managed the expectations of those who relied on me to be able to do their jobs, and was clear about when I could respond, and they were happy because I provided certainty for them, while maintaining flexibility for me. There is increased responsibility in working this way, which means you deliver when you say you're going to. That is essential to build trust in your way of working which may be out of the norm.

What I established for myself still serves me today. As I type this, we are bustling towards our deadline to get these pages to you. This means very early morning starts for me, while I balance this work, my consulting, teaching, mentoring, friendships and family. And it's the practice that I've just shared that is making all that possible.

Wellness Wheel

This is a framework based on the original created in 1976 by Dr Bill Hettler, co-founder of the National Wellness Institute. The one below builds on the original which had six segments, by including financial and environmental dimensions, which are useful additions and deserve separate consideration.

The way to work with the wheel is to answer the series of questions from each category to identify areas that perhaps need more attention. The links to these resources are in the back of the book. Although I present it here in the context of self-care, it's also a useful tool when evaluating your design work. In other words, *you can use this framework to assess the 'wellness' of your work.* It helps you design systemically and holistically. Nothing exists in isolation. Asking yourself, or your team, whether you've considered each of these dimensions in your design will help you create work that is well considered and well resolved.

If we were to take a therapeutic perspective of design, we would be ensuring every dimension in this Wellness Wheel had active consideration in the design decisions we make during the project.

The resources we've shared at the back of the book will guide you through a survey to do a self assessment using the original version of this tool.

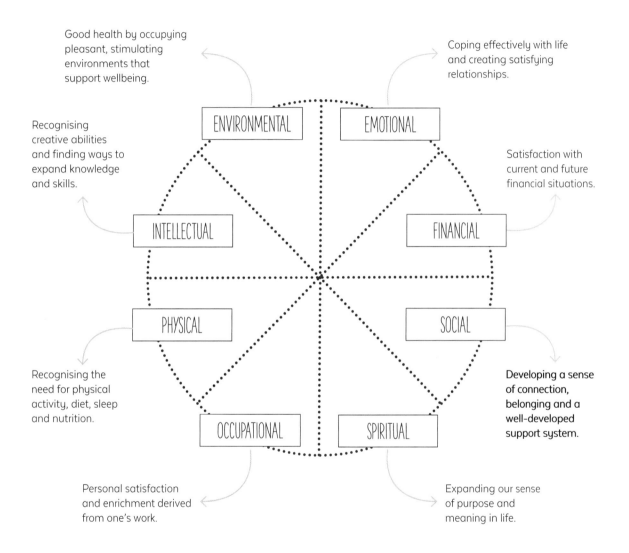

Good health by occupying pleasant, stimulating environments that support wellbeing.

Coping effectively with life and creating satisfying relationships.

Recognising creative abilities and finding ways to expand knowledge and skills.

Satisfaction with current and future financial situations.

ENVIRONMENTAL

EMOTIONAL

INTELLECTUAL

FINANCIAL

PHYSICAL

SOCIAL

OCCUPATIONAL

SPIRITUAL

Recognising the need for physical activity, diet, sleep and nutrition.

Developing a sense of connection, belonging and a well-developed support system.

Personal satisfaction and enrichment derived from one's work.

Expanding our sense of purpose and meaning in life.

FIGURE 4.1
Utilise this frame-
work to assess
the 'wellness' of
your work.

SELF CHECK-IN EMOTIONAL HEALTH

The following categories are commonly associated with emotional mastery. When you are good at these things, you will also be good at handling yourself well in most situations. When we are tired and worn out, these things becomes less available to us. These questions help you check in with yourself to help you know when you need some care.

Although they are presented in steps, you don't have to do them all in one sitting, and you don't have to do them in this order. They have been presented in this order as there is a sense of the previous needing to be present for the next to be available, but that is not always the case.

01

SIT DOWN WITH YOUR JOURNAL

Sit down with your journal, or whatever you use to capture your reflections, and answer the following questions as honestly as you can.

02

CHECK IN WITH SELF INQUIRY
The ability to engage in honest inquiry and exploration of how you are.

This is first because it is essential to be able to do the rest of the exercise. Ask yourself whether you are in a position to be able to answer the questions honestly, or whether you're too tired to even go there. This in itself is a signal for you to down tools for a bit, and get some space and time to calm your nervous system down. In a calmer state, self inquiry is more available to us.

03

SELF AWARNESS
The ability to witness yourself think, act and feel.

Example questions:

- How am I feeling? Where am I feeling it in my body?

- How have I been contributing to my family, friends, colleagues?

- How have my thoughts been lately? (Uplifting, positive, saddening, negative)

SELF ACCEPTANCE

The ability to accept (and forgive) who you are, as you are.

Example questions:

- Is there something that is bothering me? Do I know what my role was in that?
- Am I able to forgive myself for my role in that and accept I won't always get it right?
- Am I able to embrace the great work I'm doing and the positive contribution I'm making?

SELF REGULATION

The ability to modulate emotional intensity, to respond instead of react.

Example questions:

- Have I been able to remain calm in heightened emotional situations?
- Am I able to calm my thoughts to also calm my emotions?
- Do I know what to do with my body to move strong emotions through?

SELF EXPRESSION

The ability to express your truth authentically.

Example questions:

- How have I been communicating my thoughts and feelings lately?
- Are there thoughts and emotions I'm holding on to?
- Is there something I need to say to someone to let go of any emotion?

READ OVER WHAT YOU'VE CAPTURED

Have a look at your answers and see if you need to create some space for some rest and relaxation to get you back on track.

REMEMBER

The questions are here as a guide only, to give you a sense of the different categories. Depending on where you are at, what is happening in your world, you will need to ask questions that are more specific to your experience.

Care for others

When we cover this section in the Design Character course I often get mixed reviews. Some people resonate with the material, others find it unnecessary or confusing. Those who resonate with the topic have found themselves in a position of needing the kind of support I refer to. Those who don't, haven't... yet.

There are many approaches in design research in particular that are not too distant from techniques used in psychotherapy. As I continue on my journey to become a qualified somatic psychotherapist, the more I learn, the more connections I can see. In the field of mental health, there is a form of support and mentoring for therapists called 'supervision'. Now for (mostly) self-directed designers who gravitate toward this kind of work, they tend to baulk at the word. The intention that sits behind this word I think is important for the design industry to consider.

Many designers at various stages of their career are sent into situations where they need to work with vulnerable communities for example, and co-create solutions that might serve their needs better. During these sessions, if the designers are doing their job well, people they are designing with will share generously about their experiences and why they need things to be different. *These stories can be difficult to hear and difficult to work with.*

Currently there is no formal process where designers are able to seek the kind of support provided in the mental health care profession for a thorough debrief to occur. We have no in-built discipline where more experienced designers help put things into perspective, or help provide guidance and mentoring on how to proceed and how to take part in self-care disciplines. This is currently provided by line managers, or more senior designers in the team, on an ad hoc, needs basis.

As the role of human-centered design is still developing within most organisations, it is not always likely your line manager will also have a background in design.

I wonder what 'design supervision' would look like and whether you think we need it in our profession? The graduates of the Design Character course tend to prefer 'design support' rather than supervision, and I get it. If we were to create a framework, what would it look like?

DESIGN SUPPORT FRAMEWORK

Each organisation and each team is different, so it would be worth doing some thinking about what an appropriate design support framework might be for your team, or organisation. Next are four principles distilled from the clinical world that might help you create one that works.

A beneficial support framework will have the following aspects.

DESIGNER LED

The designer chooses the supervisor and determines the frequency, the purpose and the focus for each session and their own learning goals. This may need to be a supported process for early-career designers.

EXPERIENCE FOCUSED

The focus is on the experience of the designer while doing the work, whether that is the experience of working with their team, or the content of the material they need to absorb or with any relationship external to the project (client/customer/executive etc).

INTRA-PROFESSIONAL

The session is conducted by those who also have a design background and direct experience of what the designer is currently working with. The support provider may have breadth or depth (or both) in the same field.

OUTCOME FOCUSED

The support session will reflect on issues relating to, or affecting, the design practice and the delivery of end outcomes of the work.

01

WHATS MISSING?

Using the principles as a guide, think about whether there are any elements missing? If so, what are they? Think of your specific team and the work you do, what other principle might be needed to create a design support framework?

02

CUSTOMISE THE PRINCIPLES FOR YOUR ORGANISATION

Each organisation is different, and design is practised in a variety of different ways. How would each of the elements be done in practice within your organisation?

03

MAP IT OUT

Map this out in any way that makes sense to you. It could be a diagram, a set of words or something else altogether.

04

AN EXAMPLE

I've provided an example to show how I'm thinking about this. I imagine I would use a framework like the one below to support any designers in my team, who requested the support.

PURPOSE OF SESSION:
Designer defines the purpose of support session.

OUTCOME OF WORK:
Outcomes the designer is working towards with the people involved in project.

REFLECTION OR DEBRIEF:
Designer and mentor (support person) reflect on situation together and explore experience of designer.

- Uncover how designer can work through experience.
- Uncover self-support practices.
- Uncover supportive development opportunities These could be anything from breathing and self-regulation to a new competency.

CAPTURE LEARNINGS:
Designer and mentor can do this together or designer can do this separately and bring to next session.

NEXT SESSION:
These sessions happen on designers' terms. They may like to reschedule or prefer an ad-hoc/needs basis.

To sum up

With clarity and confidence comes authentic communication. This form of communication results in more effective design and creates more change. With more change come more demands on your time as the instigator of change. Establishing strong habits around work and rest, and holding them as equally essential to your wellbeing and to your ability to perform at your job, paves the road to a long and enjoyable career in design.

NEXT

Next we delve into power, boundaries and safety: the role they play in your work as a designer and the role you play in creating these for yourself, and for others.

05

POWER, BOUNDARIES & SAFETY

We engage with power consciously or subconsciously.

It is essential to build your power literacy to be effective in conducting, communicating and advocating for your work.

Boundaries help us negotiate the dynamics of power and by using the skill of setting, maintaining and honouring your boundaries, you create safety for yourself and those you design with.

In this chapter, my aim is to create an increased awareness about the role power plays in how you conceive of, deliver and communicate your work.

POWER IS PRESENT IN OUR WORK.

Power is an ever-present and ever-important topic to understand, especially in the context of participatory design work. Knowing its forms helps you negate its unintended influence.

The role of boundaries in establishing safety for yourself and others is also discussed and done so deliberately in the context of power. By the end of this chapter, you will have all you need to establish a safe, ethical design practice unique to you.

Why we need to talk about power

Designers, for a long time have understood that good can be done as a result of the process or outcome of design. Being involved in a design process can feel like a therapeutic experience for people who are sharing their experiences with a service, policy or system that is the object of redesign. That is, the process itself can achieve good outcomes. The result of this work can also have a positive impact as the grievance is removed as a result of great design work. ***However, it seems that good intentions aren't always enough.***

As designers, having accountability for the vulnerabilities and challenging experiences our processes can unearth is important. This accountability requires well thought-through frameworks that act as scaffolding to hold ourselves and participants in safety (which we'll get to a bit later in this chapter).

Knowing the power you hold is important to ensure you work with it in a sensitive way. Especially if the group of people you are working alongside represent a group who may have been exploited in such processes in the past.

Understanding power and its role in our work is critical to avoiding its unintended misuse. Without building our awareness and our literacy in power, we cannot mitigate the inadvertent consequences of wielding it clumsily.

We will leverage the great work of Goodwill, Bendor and van der Bijl-Brouwer (2021) who describe this eloquently in their article:

> "Without a deeper understanding of how the identities of and inter-relationships between stakeholders are premised in social structures that uphold structural inequality (such as norms, roles, rules, assumptions, and beliefs), designers risk reproducing existing inequities by keeping power concentrated in the hands of those who are already privileged—be it more influential stakeholders or the designers themselves. As design becomes more diffuse (Manzini, 2015), so should the power of designers." (Goodwill et al (2021) p.45).

Tension exists between our intent to share power by avoiding taking the position of 'expert' and the inherent power we hold by being the person in the room with the education and experience to facilitate such a process.

As designers, we hold a lot of power and are at the risk of not realising it, which means it is easier to misuse it. Quite often we are there at the request of another (even more powerful) person or organisation and must also be cognisant of these effects. It can get messy pretty quickly. The best work we can do in this space, is to be aware of power dynamics and relationships, to do our best to understand them and to integrate that understanding into how we design.

Types of power

Goodwill, Bendor and van der Bijl-Brouwer (Goodwill, 2021) outline five forms of power found in design practice. I share these types of power in this book with the following intentions:

1. TO INCREASE THE POWER LITERACY IN THE DESIGN INDUSTRY AND ENCOURAGE ITS INTEGRATION INTO YOUR WORK.

2. TO HELP YOU UNDERSTAND WHAT YOUR UNIQUE POSITION IS WITH RESPECT TO POWER IN YOUR PRACTICE.

3. TO BUILD OUT A ROBUST AND THOROUGH DESIGN CHARACTER.

Personally, I find this work difficult. I have a tenuous relationship with power. I have respect for it and equally I don't like it. There are few examples where I see it play out with sensitivity and grace, more often I see its abuse and misuse. It's difficult to get my head around but important that I understand it. I think you get the picture. You'll find some resources in the back of the book to further develop your understanding of this important dimension of our work. The five forms of power identified by Goodwill et al. are described next.

PRIVILEGE

The ability to influence a design process due to an unearned advantage based on social position or identity.

We start here because it informs and colours every decision we make before, during and after the design process and is largely invisible to those who have it.

The authors describe this as the ability "to influence the design process due to an unearned advantage based on their social position or identity" (Goodwill, 2021). When I read this, I let out a deep sigh. It is present in everything AND it is largely invisible to the beholder. What do I do with this information? One thing I can do is continue to do the work, be interested in these topics, incorporate reflexivity as a part of my practice and see where I can get better by understanding my own privilege.

In practice: Understand it is highly likely those with whom you work in design represent a very narrow portion of the human population. There are so many people and groups that have different lived experience, beliefs and understanding of social roles to you. Not all people share the same norms or assumptions of the world.

Be aware that the sense you and your team make will be informed by your version of the preceding dimensions which may be different to those of the people your work may be in service of.

The most straightforward approach to reducing the impact of this is to be as inclusive in the design process as possible and to keep working on developing your own awareness and understanding.

ACCESS *and*
ROLE POWER

The ability to decide who is included or excluded from a project—both those who do the work, and those who inform the work.

The decisions about who's on the project and their role, who does the recruitment, who the participants are, who's the senior designer, project leader are all examples of actions that are afforded by access and role power. This is also relevant not only to project set-up but as the design process unfolds

Design by its nature is emergent and we learn more as we move through the process. As we learn, we make different decisions about where we need to head to next. People who get to make those decisions and participate are then able to influence the work, while others may not.

And finally, this kind of power is at play at any point of convergence, when

a decision is taken, sometimes on behalf of people who aren't in the room. The authors explain these as two separate power types, I have combined them here for simplicity and brevity.

In practice: It is essential to consider who is NOT in the room when decisions are being made. It is impractical to assume that all those affected by the work will be present when decisions and judgements are being made, but it is practical to notice who is not represented and to be conscious and deliberate about proceeding with or without them present. This is better than proceeding without awareness of the implications.

The use of the word judgement is very deliberate and serves to distinguish between it and decision making. While decisions are cognitive, thought-based processes, judgements come from the body, have a feeling associated, and can be made without all the information. This is not the same as passing judge-ment about a person or situation —being judgy.

GOAL POWER

Ability to initiate and frame the design work, how problems are defined, goals are chosen and the work is structured.

This power refers to those who set the goals of the design project. The outcome of the work, the problem space and problem definition all have a significant impact on all dimensions of the design project. These include the approach that is taken, the methodologies that are used and the outcomes that guide analysis and synthesis.

If the stakeholders who have a share in goal power do NOT represent the people who will be living with the outcomes of the design project, these interests will not be present in the crucial conversations.

Going ahead with the design work, without considering the role goal power plays in the formation of the project can be risky. The designer is at risk of being unaware of the pre-existing agenda and the real issues affecting the project.

In practice: One of the most frustrating aspects of working within an agency is the common dilemma of a client asking for work to solve a problem they have already identified without consulting with the citizens/ customers/ stakeholders affected.

Seeing this through the frame of power, it can be understood as a potential misuse. To assume the client's understanding of the project goal is correct, without consulting with the group the work will be in service of, is inherently risky. Helping the client see the implications of this missed step through the lens of power can be a strong way of addressing it.

RULE POWER

Ability to establish how those involved in the project will work together. These norms determine participation and how and when knowledge is shared.

I am sure you have heard the phrase *"information is power"*. This form of power relates to the rules that govern how decisions are made about what is important, what concepts get reviewed, which ones don't, what gets shared, when and with whom. When information does get shared, it then gets interpreted and those in the room who know the rules get to decide what becomes the dominant interpretation of the work.

Rules can be as simple as how long a co-design session typically goes for, or less obvious like the norms of conduct during a critique session. There are other rules imposed, such as the language that is spoken, the jargon that is allowed and the form of participation that is required (in person, over video, all together, asynchronous etc).

In practice: There are many rules that govern how we work together, not all of them are explicit and known to everyone. For example, many designers conceive of workshop flows and formats that also fit their preferences. For example, I prefer small groups, in person and I enjoy an unstructured emergent approach. This can be fear-inducing for some people who are unsure of this way of working. They may find it unfamiliar and difficult to engage in this way due to physical, social, psychological, linguistic or cognitive reasons. Knowing that I am setting the rules of engagement for others reminds me to be understanding of their experience. This awareness affords the opening for those rules to change to accommodate different needs.

As I've mentioned earlier, it is not always possible to address all of these points, but it is always possible to try.

"*Each* UNDERESTIMATES *her own* POWER *and* OVERESTIMATES *the other's.*"

Deborah Tannen

POWER LITERACY FRAMEWORK

There is a very comprehensive list of questions in Goodwill et al., (page 55) and I have adapted these questions to fit within this exercise. The following are provided to help you become familiar with the five forms of power in your design practice and to start working more intentionally with power.

01

PRIVILEGE

1. What privilege do you have and how does it differ from those you are working with? Think specifically about the participants in your design research.

2. What advantages do you experience (that you notice) in your daily life due to your privilege? How does this inform your biases?

3. How do your biases affect how you relate to the work you are doing? There's a whole section on this in the first book, *this human*, Chapter 1 pp 12-13 and Exercise 1.2.

02

ACCESS

1. Which stakeholders are represented in your design cohort, and which are not? Notice who is missing.

2. How are different stakeholders invited into the process?

3. Will each stakeholder have similar/equal access as one another through the project or will it change? When, how, who gets to decide?

4. How much influence do you have in determining access?

04

ROLE POWER

1. What implicit hierarchy comes with the different roles on the project? How does this affect participation?

2. Do these roles challenge status quo inequities or reproduce them? Either within the design team, or as a result of the work?

3. Who will have the ability to interpret and/ or prioritise findings?

4. Is non-participation a valid option for some stakeholders?

03

GOAL POWER

1. Who/how was the project initiated? What problems, outcomes and processes have already been decided?

2. How much influence do you have on the project outcomes?

3. How might the framing of the project affect participation in the project? Who may be included/excluded as a result?

05

RULE POWER

1. What are our defined ways of working?

2. What ways of knowing, and doing, are deemed most appropriate?

3. How might these rules amplify certain voices, and dampen others?

REFLECTIVE PRACTICE IS ESSENTIAL FOR A STRONG DESIGN CHARACTER.

This is a mandatory requirement for anyone I coach or mentor. Reflection is the only way we can deepen our understanding of the role we play in our work, and increase our literacy in important influences like power.

Boundaries

We don't often talk about boundaries in the way we are about to within a design context. We might talk about a boundary condition, or a boundary object, but personal and professional boundaries are not often discussed in the context of ethical design practice. So let's get into it.

Up to this point in the book, we have covered the effect of values and attention on what you hold as important as you design. We've covered ethics and the role they play in setting the standards for your work. We've covered communication and self-care and the important intersection they have. And more recently, we've dipped our toe into the field of power and reflected on how it relates to our design practice—and now, boundaries.

BOUNDARIES ARE WHAT HELP YOU ENACT YOUR CHOICES.

They signal to those you work with what is ok, and what is not ok. When done well, boundaries keep you and others safe.

WHAT ARE THEY *and* WHY ARE THEY IMPORTANT?

Boundaries are like invisible lines in the sand. Or if I could quote Johnny Castle from Dirty Dancing, "This is my dance space, this is your dance space—I don't go into yours, you don't go into mine, you've got to hold your frame."

Boundaries are most often communicated verbally, but they can also be communicated non-verbally as you'll see in the explanations below.

There are four things to consider when working with boundaries: **setting, maintaining, enforcing and honouring.**

WHEN COMMUNICATED EFFECTIVELY, BOUNDARIES ARE HOW YOU UPHOLD YOUR STANDARDS.

SETTING BOUNDARIES

There are different boundary types and different approaches to setting them. The most important thing to remember at this point is to know what they are. **Often this is the hardest part.** Sometimes we feel like we've been taken advantage of, or not seen, or ignored, which hurts us. But what we don't know is that a boundary has inevitably been crossed and we didn't even realised we had one there!

The reflective nature of this work helps you dig deep and identify what those boundaries are for you, so you can set them to keep yourself safe and operate with authenticity.

MAINTAINING BOUNDARIES

Boundary-setting is not a one-time activity. We need to revisit and reassess our boundaries to ensure they remain supportive for our work and growth.

Sometimes we realise (as I did) that some boundaries are leftovers from a lifetime ago. A regular boundary maintenance program is needed to keep up with the changing contexts of our lives and our work.

ENFORCING BOUNDARIES

I often work with people who say they
don't like enforcing boundaries because
it feels uncomfortable. You might not
enforce your boundary because you
don't want to hurt the other person.
The choice you're actually making in
that moment is to transfer that suffering
onto yourself. And when you do that,
you end up resenting the person who
asked you to do what they needed,
which really isn't fair on them either.
You feel bad for longer, and direct
unkind emotions towards the person
who is happily going about their
business thinking that you're all
rainbows and unicorns. It is always
better, in this kind of situation, to
remind them of your boundary.

HONOURING BOUNDARIES

Just as you have the right to set
your boundaries and communicate
your needs and preferences, so do
seven billion other people we share
this planet with. Although many of
those seven billion wouldn't have
access to opportunities that afford
such discourse (yes, a bit of privilege
here too). It is just as important to
become great at perceiving where
other people's boundaries are so
you can honour theirs.

Types of boundaries

There are many different ways to view boundaries and categorise them. These relate more to a design practice. In the boundaries exercise you'll learn more about these, so here is a summary.

PHYSICAL

The way space is organised or occupied communicates the preferences of the teams working within that space. It can be used to allow people in, keep people out, to foster creativity or seriousness. Physical artefacts in the space further help uphold boundaries, 'keep quiet', 'no running', 'keep calm and...' so on. Body language also plays a role in nonverbal signals that communicates your intentions. How you hold your body, what you do or don't do, how you greet someone all establish physical boundaries around interaction.

- Space where design/work happens
- body, personal space, touch, hugs/hands
- things, tools, artefacts.

EMOTIONAL

Emotional boundaries ensure we get our needs met and contribute to us remaining strong and performing at work. These needs may be feelings of emotional safety, or feeling included or valued. We uphold these values by communicating when we are un-comfortable, when we need support or by being clear on what you will or won't tolerate in terms of behaviour toward or around you.

- Conversations you will/ won't engage in
- mentoring, support structure, asking for help
- creating opportunities for rest, space for healing.

INTELLECTUAL

The frameworks, approaches, world views you have determine what's ok and what's not ok. These are typically your preferences in how you like to work (and live). Intellectual boundaries might be crossed when someone insists you agree with their point of view and depart from your own. Remember, open-mindedness doesn't mean that you take on other people's opinions. It means you can see others' perspectives and accept that they too can exist alongside your (perhaps) opposing view.

- Ethical framework, belief structure, world view

- process, outcomes, outputs, methods

- ways of thinking, ways of working.

TIME

This is a really important one that often gets overlooked and is also caught up in the 'grind culture' I referred to earlier in the self-care section. We find it very difficult to create healthy time boundaries for ourselves, and so others find it difficult to a) know where they are and b) respect them.

- When things happen

- how long they take to happen

- how often they happen.

REMEMBER

Like everything else in life, setting and holding healthy boundaries in your work takes practice.

BOUNDARY SETTING

The following exercise is designed to help you become familiar with the different types of boundaries and help identify where you might need to establish some new ones, or reinforce some old ones.

01

FIND AN AREA OF FOCUS

Pick one area within your design practice (or work/life in general) where you think you need to assert a boundary or establish a new one. Make sure it is doable, and small and not too risky for you. It is great to start small if this is not something you are already comfortable with so you can build positive association with the action.

02

IDENTIFY CROSSED BOUNDARIES

Read through each sentence and decide which boundaries have been crossed Physical (P), Emotional (E), Intellectual (I), Time (T). Place the letter in the white box to record your result.

The workshop kit you continue to keep stocked is always depleted and never returned to its original state for you to use.

The physical area you've allocated to do your design work keeps getting taken over by other groups (including your whiteboard being wiped without your permission— THE WORST!).

Your approach to design research is changed without consultation with you to a form that doesn't meet your ethical standards.

Your team mate keeps talking to you about a personal dilemma he has with his romantic partner which leaves you feeling uncomfortable.

You have blocked out focus time
in your calendar and people keep
booking meetings over it.

03

SET A NEW BOUNDARY

Once you've identified where a boundary is not
being respected, go about setting one. Make sure
you remember to observe what changes when you
set it. Write about this in your journal, or record it
wherever you do your reflective practice.

Your client always leans in a
little too closely when speaking with
you and you hesitate to step away
as you don't want to offend.

You are exhausted and keep
saying yes to more work.

You have allocated 6:30 to 7:30am
in your personal diary for stay-at-
home yoga, but you never do it.

VISUALISING YOUR BOUNDARIES

This exercise was suggested by a student during a course and we all loved it so much, I thought I'd include it here also. This is something you can do on your own, or in a group. It is a simple visualisation exercise, and it is in its basic form here, I invite you to build on it and expand it to suit.

01 FIND A SPACE TO BE CALM

Take a moment to calm your mind, taking a few deep breaths always helps with a visualisation exercise. Try to think about a boundary you may have, whether it is a personal or professional one. You can be specific, or you may find thinking about the concept of boundaries is easier for you.

02 OBSERVE YOUR MIND

Sit with the thought and observe what is happening in your mind and your body. Sometimes we imagine a scene, or for those of us who don't think in pictures, we may hear a dialogue, or music, or particular sounds. You might feel a sensation in your body that hints at what the boundary might be like. Be patient with this step, it doesn't always come to us immediately, especially if we are not familiar with visualisation as a technique.

03 GIVE FORM TO YOUR THOUGHTS

When you feel ready, try to give form to this visualisation or experience. This might be through sharing it with someone, or sketching it on a piece of paper. It is a great exercise to do as a group as it connects us with the concept of boundaries, it gives us insight into how different people connect with the concept and enriches us as a result.

"Only the truth
of who you are,
if realised,
will set you free."

Eckhart Tolle

Safety

One realisation that changed my perception of having clear boundaries in my life and work was the realisation that when I am clear with my boundaries, *others feel safer to be with me.*

When you communicate what you need, what's ok, what's not ok and what will happen if those boundaries are not respected, people find themselves in a clear container to be themselves. They feel safe because there is certainty around how to engage with you.

When we are asked to design a solution within a challenging context, it always starts with understanding the lived experience of the situation. For people to share their experience and to do so vulnerably, safety *must* be achieved. And as the facilitator of those conversations, it is your responsibility to establish this sense of safety.

PSYCHOLOGICAL SAFETY IS THE ABILITY FOR SOMEONE TO EXPRESS THEIR TRUE THOUGHTS AND FEELINGS WITHOUT THE FEAR OF NEGATIVE CONSEQUENCES.

CONSIDERING PSYCHOLOGICAL SAFETY

We will focus on psychological safety for the rest of this section, although there are other forms of safety we could discuss. The one most relevant to our work is this one. Psychological safety is the ability for someone to express their true thoughts and feelings without the fear of negative consequences. To feel like they can make a mistake without being made to feel belittled and that it's safe for interpersonal risk-taking.

There are three important categories to consider when thinking about psychological safety:

1. SAFETY FOR YOURSELF

You achieve this by defining what your needs are and communicating them effectively (healthy boundaries).

2. SAFETY FOR YOUR TEAM

You achieve this by making the desired behaviours explicit and actively discouraging behaviour that puts psychological safety at risk.

3. SAFETY FOR YOUR PARTICIPANTS

You achieve this by establishing guidelines around privacy, confidentiality, participation and consent.

ASSESSING FOR SAFETY

Most high-performing teams have psychological safety. This is a useful diagram to help ensure you create a psychologically safe environment for great design work to happen.

SAFE TO DISCOVER

 01

UNCOVER

Use the questions with your team to gauge where everyone is in relation to the three categories.

 02

BRAINSTORM

Work with your team to create ways to address areas where people do not feel safe.

 03

EXPERIMENT

Put the interventions in place and monitor the teams progress using the same framework.

I FEEL SAFE TO...

Discover new things

Ask questions

Experiment

Learn from my mistakes

Suggest crazy ideas

SAFE TO CHALLENGE

SAFE TO COLLABORATE

I FEEL SAFE TO…	I FEEL SAFE TO…
Challenge the status quo	Engage in an unconstrained way
Speak up	Interact with colleagues
Express ideas	Have mutual access
Identify changes	Maintain open dialogue
Expose problems	Foster constructive debate

WHAT HAPPENS
when SAFETY
is NOT PRESENT

Safety and trust are joined at the hip.
People need to trust each other, the
environment and the context for
safety to be possible. When safety is
not present, people contract, hesitate
and their performance is hindered.
A study published in the Academy
of Management Journal (Detert and
Burris, 2007) showed the relative
importance of psychological safety
to employee voice.

   In other words, if people don't feel
safe, they are less likely to speak up.
One of the most critical contributors
to a fair and just design process is the
facilitation of equal expression.

   In a detailed study into Google's
workforce, Project Aristotle found
that psychological safety was the key
team norm for group performance.
(Duhig, 2016) A quote from the article
sums things up nicely:

> *'As long as everyone got a chance
> to talk, the team did well. But if
> only one person or a small group
> spoke all the time, the collective
> intelligence declined.'*

When we think of it in the context of design research and co-design, we begin to understand how critical it is for a designer to be adept at creating the conditions for psychological safety to be present. Here are a few simple things to do, that can help with this:

1. BE A PERSON, NOT YOUR ROLE

I spoke about this at length in the first book (page 116). It is ok to bring emotion and empathy into the room when you do your work. In fact, to human-centred design, it is essential. It facilitates connection and it supports the establishment of trust.

2. BE CURIOUS, NOT DEFENSIVE

People need to feel like they can voice difficult matters and not be reprimanded or find themselves in a position where they have to defend and justify their experience. *Lead with questions, not with justifications.*

3. ALLOW MISTAKES, ENCOURAGE REFLECTION

If people feel safe to make mistakes, they will feel safe to share ideas and try new things. If you want an environment of creativity, this is a key ingredient. Reflection is essential to facilitate learning, so the same mistakes are made continuously. *At Huddle we used to say, make your mistakes more interesting.*

4. ENCOURAGE SELF-AWARENESS

Developing your self-awareness is the gift that keeps on giving. Encourage this in your teams and colleagues by demonstrating your own development in this area. Increased self-awareness enables you to improve your emotional mastery of yourself, which then helps model different responses to different situations for your team and contemporaries.

To sum up

The only way we can overcome the unintended consequences of our design efforts is to continue to build our awareness and understanding of the powerful background processes that are at play as we design. Knowing the types of power you have and the role they play in your work will help you do what is within your power to mitigate these effects. These realisations and deepening understandings then require new boundaries to be set so you can communicate your preferences and needs to do great design work. By doing this work, you will create safety for yourself and for those around you.

NEXT
We bring everything together in your Design Character framework. This is a tool you can use with yourself, and your teams, forever and ever and ever.

06

REFLEXIVITY

To become better designers, we need to be disciplined at integrating all that we learn about ourselves and the world into action.

This is reflexivity.

REFLECTION ENABLES PERSONAL GROWTH.

In this chapter, we bring all the concepts we've introduced so far together.

Just like anything, ***building design character takes practice.***

We'll do this within a critical reflexivity framework you can use to direct your own development of character, and also to incorporate generally into your work.

I introduce the Design Character framework and show how it can be used as a communication and reflexivity tool, for yourself and your teams, to continue your design character development.

What is Reflexivity?

REFLECTION IS AN ESSENTIAL PRACTICE IN DESIGN.

Throughout my practice and my teaching, I advocate for designers to incorporate reflection as a key practice in their design work. The purpose of reflection is to uncover the role you play in how your work is unfolding. This awareness is not really enough though. We need to do something with this new awareness and understanding.

In my previous book, I referred to this as integration - the process of integrating knowledge into action. After reading a paper looking at critical reflexivity in the field of health promotion, I realised there is a better way to describe reflection and integration—reflexivity.

> *"Isn't it odd. We can only see our* OUTSIDES, *but nearly* EVERYTHING *happens on the* INSIDE."
>
> *Charlie Mackesy*

In a paper by Norton and Sliep (2018), a critical reflexivity framework is discussed. As I read this paper, I realised the entire book that you are reading right now is about reflexivity and how it builds character.

To understand the background elements that motivate you, that inform your standards, that guide your attention and the practice of integrating them into how you are as a designer IS reflexivity. Mind blown.

"It is an ongoing practice of testing out assumptions and intentions that takes into account how our actions are influenced by our context and how our context is, in turn, influenced by our actions." Norton and Sliep (2018).

Sounds a lot like design, doesn't it? So, it is with great delight that I show you how the work you've done so far fits neatly into this framework that has been developed by the authors. First, let's get familiar with their work.

Critical Reflexivity

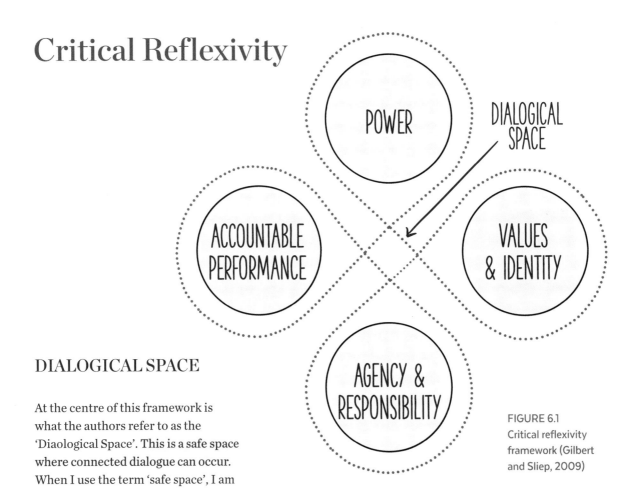

POWER

DIALOGICAL SPACE

ACCOUNTABLE PERFORMANCE

VALUES & IDENTITY

AGENCY & RESPONSIBILITY

FIGURE 6.1
Critical reflexivity
framework (Gilbert
and Sliep, 2009)

DIALOGICAL SPACE

At the centre of this framework is
what the authors refer to as the
'Diaological Space'. This is a safe space
where connected dialogue can occur.
When I use the term 'safe space', I am
referring to many different elements
coming together simultaneously, such
as presence, listening, non-judgement,
empathy and trust. We just spent an
entire chapter exploring safety, so it is
hopefully clear how this maps to this
framework. There are some important
points the authors make about this
space that are worth noting,
summarised as follows:

1. THE SPACE IS FACILITATED

In this study, it is the educators who facilitate this space for students. In our work, it is the designer who is doing this role. The facilitation of a dialogical space like this requires certain conditions to be established and maintained. I have already mentioned some of these, but I want to emphasise 'no judgement' in particular, which the authors refer to as 'critical acceptance'. I like this term more. This establishes a clear environment of respect for diverse perspectives and experiences, and creates the conditions for learning and reflexivity.

2. THE SPACE IS INTENTIONAL

There is a clear intention established when creating this kind of space, that is one of learning and integration. To facilitate this process, people need to feel safe, be open-minded (and open-hearted, I would add), and willing to share their experiences. Clarity about the intention of the space requires boundary setting for people to feel safe within it. The role of the facilitator is to be clear about what this space is in aid of, and to ensure people consent to participating in an intentional way.

   As an aside: there was a lot I couldn't squish into this book, one important section was about consent, so I have provided some resources in the back for you to explore. Consent is a huge consideration when traversing the terrains of power and ethics.

3. THE SPACE IS EGALITARIAN

Power is authentically acknowledged and shared in such spaces to ensure that social status, rank and role do not influence participants' abilities to contribute and share. The designer, stakeholders and participants are all on equal footing and all stories, opinions and commentary hold equal importance. It is important to also acknowledge that while this is the ideal scenario, these perceptional hierarchies exist within us, and are sometimes difficult to shift— those tensions and inequalities must not be ignored when present.

4. THE SPACE WELCOMES STORIES

Rather than reporting-out on experience, using facts and figures, participants are invited to use story-telling, poetry and other creative methods of form-giving to share. While the paper refers to the use of story and poetry, the methods in design can extend to include many 'making methods' including drawing, painting, sculpting and constructing.

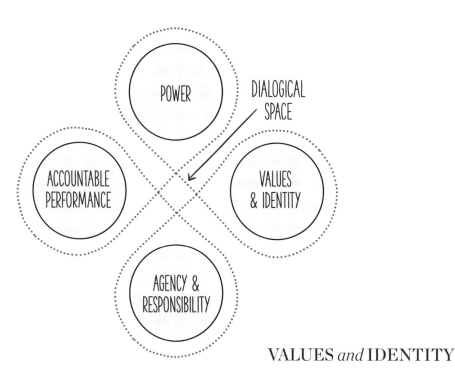

POWER

DIALOGICAL SPACE

ACCOUNTABLE PERFORMANCE

VALUES & IDENTITY

AGENCY & RESPONSIBILITY

VALUES *and* IDENTITY

I find identity and personality very interesting and how they impact our actions (conscious and unconscious). If you want to dive deeper, I have included some resources for you to explore further (eg. Oyserman, 2012).

It is important to acknowledge that both identity and personality play a very influential role in this work. In my work on values, I took an approach looking for a universal understanding of values to act as an anchor, while building the other parts of your design character. The work explored by the authors of this paper on reflexivity approached values differently. They took a view that values are understood 'in terms of collective negotiation and communal participation'.

POWER

In this model of reflexivity, participants are encouraged to examine how power operates in their lives on a personal, societal and political level. This examination and reflection seeks to advance understanding of power in their lives, rather than seeking to dismantle it. Typically any exploration of power leads to questioning certain forms of power and their influence on the individual. Just like we did in the previous chapter, seeking to understand the role of power in design. This then leads to questions about values and how you situate yourself within those power structures.

AGENCY *and* RESPONSIBILITY

The process of uncovering what you value, your standards and the aware-ness of choices that shape who you are, builds agency. **With this agency comes responsibility**. This is another theme that ducks and weaves throughout this book. When you become a person who is impactful and influential in the field of design, there is an equal responsibility that comes with it, (if you seek to accept it, of course). I always think of Spiderman at this point—I'm sure you have heard this many times, but here it is again:

WITH GREAT POWER COMES GREAT RESPONSIBILITY.

ACCOUNTABLE PERFORMANCE

This is a beautiful phrase to me.

It is essential to all ongoing personal development. Through my coaching practice, I have come to realise there are some people who are good at incorporating their thoughts and words into action. They begin experimenting with different ways of doing to reflect their new ways of thinking. Others find crossing this bridge more treacherous and remain in the thought and insight realm. There is an incremental ratcheting that occurs when we put things into action through accountable performance that supercharges our own development. When we cannot make this transition, we can find ourselves in a loop of doing more courses, seeking more coaches and not seeing the fruits of that effort.

> '[Accountable performance] requires living the preferred story, putting words into accountable action or walking the talk.' Sliep and Norton, 2016.

To see how these all connect and fit together, I've mapped the content in this book to this framework. This is exciting because it is also a methodology you can use to hold sessions to facilitate the kind of process required to explore design character.

FIGURE 6.2
Critical Reflexivity
Framework mapped
to the content in
this book.

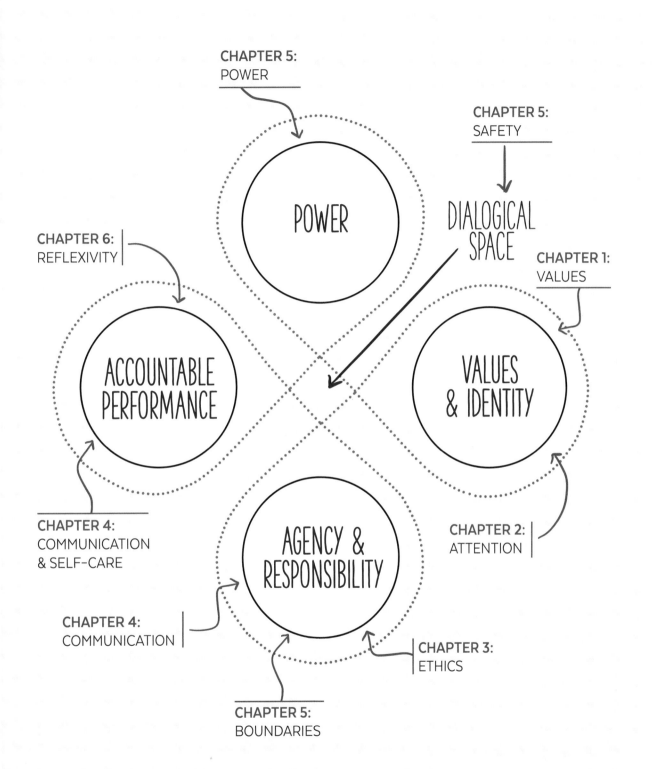

CHAPTER 5:
POWER

CHAPTER 5:
SAFETY

POWER

DIALOGICAL
SPACE

CHAPTER 6:
REFLEXIVITY

CHAPTER 1:
VALUES

ACCOUNTABLE
PERFORMANCE

VALUES
& IDENTITY

CHAPTER 4:
COMMUNICATION
& SELF-CARE

CHAPTER 2:
ATTENTION

CHAPTER 4:
COMMUNICATION

AGENCY &
RESPONSIBILITY

CHAPTER 3:
ETHICS

CHAPTER 5:
BOUNDARIES

Why is Reflexivity important to design?

DESIGN BY ITS VERY NATURE IS AN EMERGENT AND REFLEXIVE PRACTICE.

We have been discussing reflexivity in the context of personal development, but what about in the context of design? Design, by its very nature, is an emergent and reflexive practice. We take action to learn, integrate and take new action. This is what makes it a beautiful methodology for complex contexts and a sound risk mitigation approach.

Reflexivity helps an emergent practice like design.

It solidifies your next step by integrating what you've learned into action.

But, without the practice and capability of reflexivity, the most important element can be missing. That is, actually doing something different as a result of that learning. Design is reflexive. It has to be, because it is the process of bringing something into reality. If we stay in the thought space, we are not directly affecting change in the material realm. This is where our shared interactions are, where services and products intersect with our lives.

It is also possible to do design without reflexivity. At the risk of sounding cynical, it is possible to continue to create the same things over and over again, without thinking about the systemic impact; continuing to unconsciously perpetuate practices you may not even agree with, staying at the current level of mastery. That is possible. But perhaps not desirable.

If your desire is to participate in the creation of shared realities that represent who you want to be in the world, and how you envision that world to be with others, then reflexivity HAS to be present in your work—within yourself and with others.

HOW TO ESTABLISH A REFLEXIVE PRACTICE FOR YOURSELF

The biggest difference between a reflective practice and a reflexive one is the latter is a practice that integrates learning into action. It tracks what it is you are actually doing differently, learns from the implications of that difference and then integrates the learning into practice. I use action experiments to progress my own practice and try new things. I also use them when I teach, to enable deep learning opportunities for students.

01

ESTABLISH A METHOD OF SELF-REFLECTION

Self-awareness and insight are only possible through reflecting on your behaviour and on events in your life. If you are committed to improving yourself and your practice, you must have a reflective practice. There are many different methods of self-reflection—personally, I use a journal—and I'll share a few principles that help them be effective:

TRUST YOURSELF
Trust that the process of reflecting will work for you and give you access to insights about your behaviour that will enhance how you are in the world and your work as a designer.

BE HONEST
It is important to create the opportunity for some honesty. If you feel bad about an interaction, own up to your part in it. It is important to be honest so you have access to the learning that sits within it.

KEEP TRACK
Make sure you record your reflections in some way. If you don't like writing, create some audio or video recordings of yourself.

TAKE YOUR TIME
Reflection is a contemplative practice. It is something that needs some space around it and requires time to get into the deep material.

BE GENTLE
While being honest, it is also important to be gentle with yourself. Show yourself the compassion you would afford another who was sharing the same information with you.

NOTICE PATTERNS
Read back over your reflections and notice patterns. Use your abilities of analysis and synthesis to notice themes.

02

CREATE ACTION EXPERIMENTS — INCORPORATE A REFLEXIVE PRACTICE

From the themes you have extracted, construct little micro experiments to enact the insight. For example a theme might be defensiveness around critique of your work, or emotional self-regulation when triggered around ethical process. Create an action experiment that requires you to do a small thing differently next time you find yourself in the same situation. It can be as small as taking a deep breath or a sip of water before responding.

Here are a few tips to create useful action experiments:

1. **Keep them small and easy**
   This is crucial because if they are too risky, scary and elaborate, you won't do it.

2. **Keep them noticeable**
   Initially it is preferable if they result in a different action, either within yourself or others. For example, If you just think differently without communicating the change, you might not see an obvious difference in the situation.

3. **Keep them short-term**
   Best not to plan a multi-year longitudinal study on the effects of taking a pause before you speak when triggered. I would suggest you run them for about a week and make sure you pay attention to what's happening around you and in you when the activity is live.

Obviously the change we are seeking is long-term within you, but the action experiment itself needs to be short so you can see some progress.

03

RINSE AND REPEAT

Use your established reflective practice to record what you notice that is different. Your reflection might be that you feel differently at work, or you are noticing less conflict or more attention, or your work seems to be flowing a little easier lately. Use the principles listed in Step 1 to capture what you're noticing about your action experiments.

YOU CAN HAVE A REFLECTIVE PRACTICE WITHOUT REFLEXIVITY, BUT NOT THE OTHER WAY AROUND.

The Design Character framework

YOUR DESIGN CHARACTER IS NEVER FINISHED.

Because of reflexivity, you have the opportunity to continue to develop your character as you and your world changes. Your design character becomes defined and formed as you do the work to become fluent in your values, to understand how your attention and energy flow, to become practiced at communicating your position and approach to things, clarify your ethical approaches and negotiate power and safety. Phew, that's a lot. But it's worth it.

Your design character is what emerges from this work.

The Design Character framework is a tool aimed at helping you continue to hone how you express your character. Our ability to communicate where we stand is facilitated through language. This framework is a reflexivity tool that brings together what we've been exploring in a coherent way so you can talk about it easily.

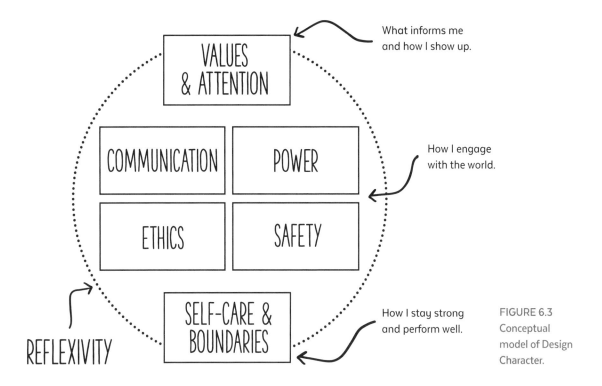

VALUES & ATTENTION

What informs me and how I show up.

COMMUNICATION

POWER

How I engage with the world.

ETHICS

SAFETY

SELF-CARE & BOUNDARIES

How I stay strong and perform well.

REFLEXIVITY

FIGURE 6.3
Conceptual
model of Design
Character.

Above is the conceptual model. At the top we have Values and Attention. Understanding your values, how they motivate you and direct your attention helps you communicate what informs you and describes *how you show up* in your work. Communication, Power, Ethics and Safety all combine to define *how you engage* with others throughout your work. And the Self-Care and Boundaries section describes *how you stay healthy and strong* so you can continue to perform well.

If we go back to the conversation between Charlie and Billy earlier in the book, when Charlie meets Billy to talk through her thoughts about the effective use of co-design in the project, she will be able to use this framework to do some prep for that meeting. Reconnecting with her values and understanding why she feels her values are being challenged. She can also reconnect with her ethical framework and help Billy understand why doing co-design properly (or not) is an ethical issue.

DESIGN CHARACTER FRAMEWORK

VALUES 01

The values I align with most are:

The values I align with least are:

COMMUNICATION 03

My approach to communicating my practice is:

The conversations I need to practice are:

POWER 04

I am aware the power I hold in this work is:

This is how I intend to genuinely share power:

ETHICS 05

My design practice is informed by these ethical principles:

An explanation of how to fill in these boxes can be found on the following pages.

SELF-CARE 07

I have the following approach to self-care in place:

This is what I do when I need support:

ATTENTION 02

My attention will be naturally drawn to:

I need to pay deliberate attention to:

The answers to these questions define what informs you, and reminds you of what your blind spots might be.

SAFETY 06

I create safety in my work by:

This is the framework I use to support for others:

The answers to these questions define how you engage with others as you practise design.

BOUNDARIES 08

These are the boundaries I have in place around my practice:

This is how I choose assert my boundaries when challenged.

The answers to these questions define how you stay strong and continue to perform well in your role.

The next exercise talks you through how to work with the framework. Following that I'll share some other scenarios where it might prove useful.

HOW TO USE THE DESIGN CHARACTER FRAMEWORK

There are many tools out there like the business model canvas, or the value proposition canvas, or the how to tie your shoelace canvas. Well, this looks similar... but it's a framework. This is how you work with it.

01

DOWNLOAD THE FRAMEWORK

Head to the this human community and download the framework from the worksheets section. The link to this can be found in the Resources section.

02

START WITH VALUES

Using the exercises and resources described in Chapter 1, work through the values survey and answer the questions in the framework. Listing the values you align with most and least serves to remind you what you will tend to be motivated by, and what you might overlook.

03

COMPLETE ATTENTION SECTION

The attention section is contextual, so when you are thinking about the answers to these questions, think about the current project you are working on or the organisation you are working within. I like to do this at a detailed level, it could even be the phase of a project so you can create an action experiment around how you might pay attention to the blind spots you've realised you might have.

04

COMMUNICATION

There were a couple of communication approaches that were introduced in this book and plenty of others in the first book. Have a think about what type of approach you might need (again, in your context) to be able to communicate your practice. It might be useful to review the 'it', 'relationship', 'me' approach, or the one outlined in Exercise 4.1.

Use this section to list the conversation types you need to improve. For example, it might be when you need to advocate for an unpopular view point, or negotiate for more time or money. Use this as a way to create action experiments to try new ways to improve, feel comfortable and get the results.

05

POWER

Completing this section will help build your own power literacy and also, that of others. When you are clear about the role power plays in your work, then you are able to talk about it with clarity and confidence. This then helps others build the same form of literacy and a shared awareness and language and so, action can happen.

06

ETHICS

In this section you list your own ethical framework that you created while completing the exercises in Chapter 3. There are a few examples we've provided in the Resources section and many more out there. Ideally, these principles will speak to you specifically and sit in alignment with your values.

07

SAFETY

This section covers creating safety for yourself and for others, and also asks that you describe the support framework you will use through your work. In Chapter 4, Exercise 4.3 guides you through a process of creating your own version of a 'design supervision' or support framework. This is what you will include in this section, in addition to how you intend to create safety for yourself and others.

08

SELF CARE

In Exercise 4.2 there is a framework for you to check in with yourself about your emotional health. As a result of this check-in, you might create some self-care practices that are always present in your life, or you might choose to do it situationally.

Knowing when you need support and what to do when you identify that for yourself is also critical to self-care. It is easy to forget about what to do when we need help. Having this written down in this section as a reminder is very useful in times of distracted stress.

09

BOUNDARIES

In exercise 5.2 you thought about the boundaries you need to put in place and those you need to uphold and maintain. The output of that exercise can be used to fill out this section. Reminding yourself of how you are going to assert those boundaries is really helpful when you are feeling vulnerable and perhaps avoiding having the conversation. It's like a gift from your future self.

NOTE

Parts of this framework can be used in workshop briefing meetings where you might pull some elements of the framework out to guide a discussion and make some decisions about the approach with the team.

To sum up

WITHOUT REFLEXIVITY WE ARE UNABLE TO PROGRESS OUR MASTERY IN OUR FIELD.

The link between having an insight, and changing our behaviour is action. Without action we cannot change our experience of ourselves and our work, nor can we change the perception of others. The Design Character framework is a tool to assist you in continuing this work, and to be a support for you when you need a gentle reminder of who you are and what you are capable of.

NEXT

In my first book, *this human*, I cover the design process from Insight to Delivery. The focus is on how to BE a designer throughout this process. In the next chapter, we'll see how these two books relate to, and support one another, and you.

07

A WORD ON
THIS HUMAN

There are plenty of exercises in the first book of this series —*this human: how to be the person designing for other people*—to support you as you define your design character.

I have mapped these exercises to the Design Character framework to act as a quick reference guide. You will find an added richness and pragmatism when you incorporate these exercises into your enquiry.

07

This chapter links the pragmatism of the previous book, with the deep contemplation of this one.

As you have turned the pages in this book, diving deeper into your design character, you might be starting to see the exercises contained in the first book in a new light.

Many of those exercises can be used to help with the practical nature of this work. I have collated a list of exercises and mapped them to the Design Character framework to help you make those connections, do the work and share it with your teams. Each exercise has a brief introduction and a description of how it can be used with the intention to do design character work.

NOTE

This Chapter relies on you also having a copy of the first book. If you don't have one, you might find the correlations interesting anyway. If you'd like to purchase a copy, all the information for how to do that are at the back of the book.

The work

To get better at anything, we need exercises, practise and ideally a coach, and perhaps even a trainer. I remember back to my tennis days, Graeme was my coach and Craig was my trainer. Graeme focussed on what was happening on the court, while Craig had me doing all sorts of weird and wacky things to build my fitness, agility and strength. This work is no different.

There are plenty of books that focus on coaching you in design—on the court. The *this human* series is about the training you need to do off the court, to become an amazing designer.

In this book, we focussed on the training needed to clarify and strengthen your character as it plays out in the field of design. This chapter is like a training manual. It draws links between the exercises shared in the first book and the awareness and insight that you are cultivating by doing the work outlined in this book.

I have mapped some exercises to the conceptual model of design character introduced in the previous chapter. The purpose of this is to connect you with the context within which you can use the exercises.

This work is contemplative and reflexive. The exercises created in *this human* are highly contextual and can be adapted by you to suit many different applications. In the next few pages, I hope to demonstrate how you can use the resources shared in this book, and the previous book, to support your design practice in vast and varied ways.

FIGURE 7.1
**DESIGN CHARACTER:
A CONCEPTUAL MODEL**

Conceptual model of the
exploration required to
uncover design character

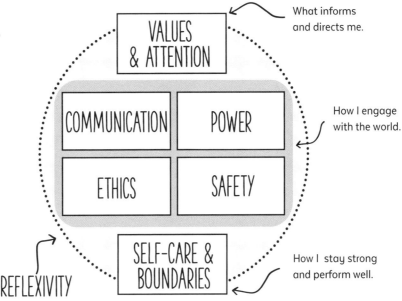

As you may have guessed by now, I love a good model. Something that simplifies and contextualises abstract, complex concepts into a form that is memorable is a welcome addition to the world inside my brain. Here it is again for your reference.

The exercises identified from the first book have been mapped to the three outcomes on the right of the model:

1. What informs and directs me
2. How I engage with the world
3. How I stay strong and perform well.

The exercises were introduced in a slightly different context in the first book. I intend to ground the application of these exercises in the work of cultivating design character. Hopefully this also demonstrates the 'Swiss Army knife' nature of the exercises.

On the following spread, you'll see all the exercises and associated page numbers mapped to this conceptual framework. I suggest marking this page so you can easily come back to it later to reference the page numbers.

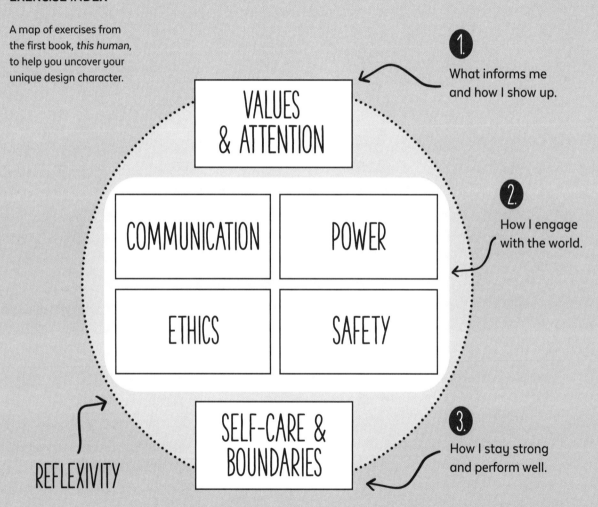

FIGURE 7.2
EXERCISE INDEX

A map of exercises from
the first book, *this human*,
to help you uncover your
unique design character.

VALUES
& ATTENTION

COMMUNICATION

POWER

ETHICS

SAFETY

SELF-CARE &
BOUNDARIES

REFLEXIVITY

1. What informs me
and how I show up.

2. How I engage
with the world.

3. How I stay strong
and perform well.

THIS HUMAN
EXERCISES

1.

THESE EXERCISES DEEPEN YOUR INSIGHT INTO HOW YOU OPERATE

2.

THIS MATERIAL STRENGTHENS YOUR ABILITY TO ENGAGE WITH THE WORLD.

3.

THIS MATERIAL HELPS YOU LOOK AFTER YOURSELF AND YOUR TEAMS.

What informs and directs me

VALUES ARE UNIVERSAL, BELIEFS ARE CONTEXTUAL.

There has been a significant and necessary focus on values throughout this book. By now you will see the fundamental role they play in informing how you design. In the first book, we cover beliefs and biases and show you ways to work with them. It is important to see how these are connected with your values and how they influence where you direct your attention.

THE DIFFERENCE
BETWEEN VALUES
and BELIEFS

In this book, we focussed on a universal view of values. In this sense, values don't change depending on context. Beliefs begin as assumptions that we hold to be true, and can be externally or internally generated. Typically they are related to experiences you've had in the past. A belief assumes what has happened in the past will also apply in the future. Collectively, beliefs affect our character and behaviour, and so are inter-related. When left unchecked, beliefs can influence our values. This is why working with beliefs is essential, so you can keep them up to date and relevant to your current context.

There is also an exercise that describes the difference between findings and insights. I have included it in this section as *values are also motivations.* They drive our behaviour and direct our attention. When we dig deeper in our research, we can drop below what is observable behaviour and begin to gain insight into what is driving that behaviour.

Often there will be values held deeply by those you are designing with or for that can explain certain behaviours. This is a useful connection for you to make when you're working with your own values.

Links to first book:

FURTHER READING:
Beliefs and Being **p7**

EXERCISES:
Working with beliefs
—Exercise 1.1 **p10-11**

Difference between
Findings and Values
—Exercise 1.10 **p36**

THE LINK BETWEEN ATTENTION *and* BIAS

We are naturally drawn to things we value, we privilege these things in our lives and so we have bias. Sometimes this bias is conscious and sometimes it is not. Unconscious bias is one of the most important tendencies we need to be aware of as designers. We need to create a way to continuously uncover 'blind spots' we would otherwise ignore, miss, under-represent or treat unfairly.

The section on biases provides a pathway for you to uncover your own, further understand the nature of them and a way to work with them. This work, in combination with understanding attention types and how to consciously direct your attention, combines beautifully to avoid adding to your bias collection.

To further develop your understanding of attention and focus, the first book also covers the difference between where your attention is drawn towards, and where your focus ought to be. While understanding your biases will give you a sense of 'what' you need to pay attention to, learning how to control your attention and focus is about 'how' to do it.

Links to first book:

EXERCISE:
Overcoming Bias
—Exercise 1.2 **p13**

FURTHER READING:
Owning your
Biases **p12**

Energy and
Will **p143**

How I engage with the world

YOU CANNOT HAVE IMPACT IN THE WORLD IF YOU ARE UNABLE TO CONNECT PEOPLE WITH YOUR WORK.

The chapters in this book on Communication, Safety, Power and Ethics are there to support you in deciding how you want to do that. There are many exercises, in addition to what has been provided in this book, to further deepen your capability to do this.

THE IMPORTANCE *of* COMMUNICATION

In both books, I have spent a lot of time discussing the role of communication in design. In this book about design character, we drew the connection between clarity, confidence, communication and self-care. Hopefully this will support you to create the disciplines to continue to communicate powerfully and with conviction, regardless of the resistance you may encounter.

In the first book, there is a section on asking the right questions and how different forms of questions provide different conversational outcomes. The Communication Directions model provides the opportunity to be more considered about what you communicate and to whom, and the

4Cs of Communication supports you to consider the elements that need to be present within you to build connection and be effective as a communicator.

If we just focussed on the speaking part of communication, we'd only be considering half the equation. This is why there are several pages focussed on listening. The Listening Channels are introduced, as well as the concept of listening to listening, which helps you identify where someone is listening from (or what channel), which then enables you to change how you communicate so you can tune into their channel.

Links to first book:
EXERCISES:
Asking the right questions
—Exercise 2.8 **p71**

Communication Directions
—Exercise 3.1 **p83**

The 4Cs of Communication
—Exercise 3.3 **p90**

Human Connections
—Exercise 4.2 **p118**

Listening Channels
—Exercise 3.7 **p98**

Listening to Listening
—Exercise 3.8 **p102**

FURTHER READING:
Listening Channels **p96**

DESIGNING *to* PREVENT UNINTENDED CONSEQUENCES

We have touched on ethics and provided a method to help you establish your own ethical framework. There are some exercises that help to draw your attention to what constitutes a well-resolved design. The process of considering your design through this lens also provides a way to ensure that ethical considerations are present. It brings a conscious and deliberate practice to considering how 'complete' your work is.

Considering the shadow scenario is another method to ensure you have spent time directing appropriate attention to unintended consequences. The Shadow Scenario method is described in the context of some work I did in considering aid distribution to displaced people during the Syrian refugee crisis. It demonstrates how we tend to focus on the idealistic version

of the systems and services that we design, thereby meaning the results of our work are not resilient to malicious intent, which is unfortunately a reality we must consider in complex systems that involves humans.

The feedback and critique process embedded in design is essential to achieve work that is well resolved, well considered and as robust and resilient as possible. To provide this direction and support effectively, we need to be deliberate in how we provide and receive feedback and how we design and hold critique sessions.

Most of the time, the people we invite into these sessions are not versed in the etiquette and approach around effective critique. There are three exercises that can help you set up these discussions so people feel safe and that the feedback gleaned from participants is constructive and moves the design forward.

Links to first book:

EXERCISES:
Attributes of a well resolved design
—Exercise 7.4 **p188**

Considering the Shadow Scenario
—Exercise 6.3 **p170**

Blissful Critique
—Exercise 3.5 **p94**

Giving great feedback
—Exercise 3.6 **p95**

Be mindful of judgements
—Exercise 1.5 **p19**

FURTHER READING:
Embracing Duality **p167**

INTERACTING *with* POWER *and* AUTHORITY

This book on design character, focusses on building your power literacy in the context of design and designing. Its aim is to build awareness of the different forms of power and how to work consciously with them in your practice. The focus in the first book is about building your own confidence and self-authority in your work. It covers the challenges we might face when we feel we need our work to be constantly validated or when we need to hold our ground against someone who might have more power and authority than we do.

Links to first book:

EXERCISE:
Own your Authority
—Exercise 5.5 **p148**

FURTHER READING:
Confidence and
Authority **p147**

How I stay strong and perform well

The final chapter of the first book focusses on delivery. It is pragmatic, grounded and talks about determination, persistence, grit and commitment. The self-care section of this book focusses on what you need to be paying attention to within yourself so you can do all the things espoused in that final chapter. There are a few specific exercises I'd like to draw your attention to.

THE ROLE *of* SELF–CARE *in* DELIVERY

At Huddle we talked about super-powers and created a way to uncover them in Huddlers and incorporate them into their mastery plans. While superpowers are wonderful to have, they also come with their associated kryptonite. I shared my own self-care journey with you earlier on page 106, Care of Self. A major contributor to that situation in my life was actually one of my superpowers, which is my wilful determination and commitment to my work. It is dangerously strong and can push me beyond my limits and what is healthy. Thankfully, I now have the disciplines in place to prevent that from happening, but it is a constant process to maintain it as an ongoing and conscious consideration.

OUR GREATEST STRENGTH CAN ALSO BE OUR GREATEST WEAKNESS.

Self-awareness is key in this regard.

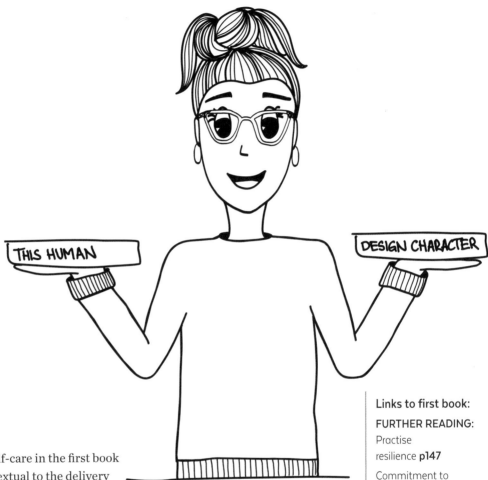

The focus on self-care in the first book is very much contextual to the delivery phase of a project; when the rubber hits the road and timelines are whooshing toward you at an ever-increasing pace.

It is a section that reminds us that taking care of yourself is a responsible stance to take when you want to ensure your work is the highest quality it can be.

It also includes the important reminder that those you are working with are people too. And the first book includes an exercise to help you understand what they might need at this stage in the process.

Links to first book:

FURTHER READING:
Practise resilience **p147**

Commitment to yourself **p180**

Commitment to your team **p181**

EXERCISE:
Commitment to people —Exercise 7.1 **p183**

The purpose of *this human* content is to continue to build and strengthen the internal infrastructure that guides everything you do in the world.

This chapter helps build the connective tissue between design character work, and how to bring that character into the world through your impactful design work.

REFERENCES
and RESOURCES

These are the references I mentioned throughout the book.

The links to all the resources (and these references) are kept up to date on my website. Use the QR code to access these links online at https://thishuman.com/resources-and-references

PREFACE
McGilchrist, I (2009) The Master and his Emissary. Yale University Press. ISBN-0-300-14878-X

INTRODUCTION
Nelson, H. and Stolterman, E. (2012) The Design Way: Intentional change in an unpredictable world (p.189). MIT Press.

CHAPTER 1: VALUES
Schwartz, S. H. (2012). An Overview of the Schwartz Theory of Basic Values. Online Readings in Psychology and Culture, 2(1). http://dx.doi.org/10.9707/2307-0919.1116

CHAPTER 2: ATTENTION
DeGangi, Georgia and Porges, Stephen. (1990). Neuroscience Foundations of Human Performance. Rockville, MD: American Occupational Therapy Association Inc.

Desbordes G, Negi LT, Pace TWW, Wallace BA, Raison CL and Schwartz EL (2012) Effects of mindful-attention and compassion meditation training on amygdala response to emotional stimuli in an ordinary, non-meditative state. Front. Hum. Neurosci. 6:292. doi: 10.3389/fnhum.2012.00292

Hawkins, D. R (2012) Power vs Force: The Hidden Determinants of Human Behaviour. Hay House. ISBN-13:9781401945077

Jabr, F (2012) Does Thinking Really Hard Burn More Calories?, Scientific American—Neuroscience, accessed 2 April, 2022 https://www.scientificamerican.com/article/ thinking-hard-calories

McGilchrist, I (2009) The Master and his Emissary. Yale University Press. ISBN-0-300-14878-X

CHAPTER 3: ETHICS
Acaroglu, Leyla (2016, Sep 1) How design design us—Part 1: The Silent Social Scripter. Medium. Retrieved April 2022 from https://medium.com/disruptive-design/how-design-designs-us-part-1-6583a9b61b57#.izqz695wu

Beard, M and Longstaff, S A (2018) Ethical Principles for Technology. The Ethics Centre, Sydney.

Nelson, H. and Stolterman, E. (2012) The Design Way: Intentional change in an unpredictable world (p.189). MIT Press.

Picard, Michael (2009) This is not a book: Adventures in popular philosophy. Crows Nest, NSW. Allen & Unwin.

Senova, M (2017) This Human: how to be the person designing for other people (p131). BIS Publishers.

Wikimedia Foundation, (2022, May 14) Feminist Ethics, Wikipedia. Retrieved 12 June 2022 from https://en.wikipedia.org/ wiki/Feminist_ethics

CHAPTER 4: COMMUNICATION & SELF-CARE
Cave, N (2022, April) Issue #190. The Red Hand Files. Retrieved May, 2022 from https://www.theredhandfiles.com/do-you-still-believe-in-us

Hettler, B (1976) Six Dimensions of Wellness Model. Retrieved May 2022 from https://www.nationalwellness.org

Kofman, F (2014) Conscious Business: How to build value through values. Sounds True, Boulder, Colorado.

Steven Pressfield (2012) Turning Pro: tap your inner power and create your life's work. Black Irish Entertainment LLC.

Senova, M (2017) This Human: how to be the person designing for other people (70-105; 107-123). BIS Publishers.

CHAPTER 5: POWER, BOUNDARIES & SAFETY
Detert, J. R and Burris, E. J (2007) Leadership behaviour and employee voice: Is the door really open? Academy of Management Journal 2007, Vol. 50, No. 4, 869–884.

Duhig, C. (2016, Feb 25) What Google Learned from its Quest to Build the Perfect Team. The New York Times Magazine. Retrieved May 2022 from https://www. nytimes.com/ 2016/02/28/magazine/what-google-learned-from-its-quest-to-build-the-perfect- team.html

Goodwill, M., Bendor, R., van der Bijl-Brower, M (2021) Beyond Good Intentions: Towards a Power Literacy Framework for Service Designers, International Journal of Design, 15(3), p45-59.

Senova, M (2017) This Human: how to be the person designing for other people (12-13). BIS Publishers.

CHAPTER 6: REFLEXIVITY
Mackesy, C. (2019) The boy, the mole, the fox and the horse. Penguin Random House, UK. ISBN 9781 52910 510 0

Norton, L and Sliep, Y. (2018) A critical reflexive model: Working with life stories in health promotion education. South African Journal of Higher Education 32(3): 45-63. http:// dx.doi.org/10.20853/32-3-2523

CHAPTER 7: A WORD ON THIS HUMAN
Senova, M (2017) This Human: how to be the person designing for other people. BIS Publishers.

INDEX

A

accountability and performance, 162, 166

agency and responsibility, 162, 166

alignment, 5, 55, 68, 177

attention, 27–39
  bias and, 190
  energy and, 31, 50
  role in directing design, 30, 44
  types of, 32
    divided, 35
    mindful, 36–7
    selective, 34
    sustained, 33
  values and, 31, 49, 188

awareness, xi, 17, 29, 42
  of self, 43, 116, 153, 170

B

beliefs, 9, 56, 188–9

boundaries, 138–147
  boundary setting exercise, 144–5
    see also—exercises
  enforcing of, 141
  honouring of, 141
  importance of, 139
  maintaining of, 140
  setting of, 140
  types of, 142–3
    emotional, 142
    intellectual, 143
    physical, 142
    time, 143
  visualising exercise, 146
    see also—exercises
  within a design context, 138, 142

C

circumplex, 8, 14
  the schwartz values circumplex model 10
    see also—values

clarity and confidence, 85–87, 109
  conflict of, 87

communication, 83–105, 192
  authentic, 122
  difficult conversations, 87–104
    anatomy of, 89–101
    having *better* difficult conversations, 104
      see also—exercises
  importance of, 193
  trust and, 95

D

delivery, 7, 120, 196
    see also—self care

design
  boundaries within, 138
  ethical, 57
  human-centred, 119
  learning domains, xiv
  paradox of, 77, 79
  purpose, 68
  reflection, 157
  reflexivity, 160–163, 168
  shadow, 77
  unconscious, xi, 30, 76
  unintended consequences, 154, 194

design character, ix
  conceptual model, 185
  definition of, xiv
  energy and, 43
  ethics and, 55
  framework, xiv, 172–175
    see also—frameworks
  how to use design character framework, 176
    see also—exercises
  power and, 130
  reflection and, 137, 159
  values and, 4

design practice, 45, 67, 142, 136, 184

dialogical space, 162
    see also—reflexivity

E

empathy, 17, 97, 153, 162

energy, 31, 40–45, 50
  definition of, 40
  relevant to design, 44
  types of, 41–43
    emotional, 42
    intellectual, 41
    physical, 43
    relational, 43

ethics, 53–80

absence of, 76–7
  critical reflection, 56
  definition of, 56
  ethical framework, 62, 67
    see also—frameworks
  ethical theory, 62
  in the context of design, 55, 66
  types of, 58–61
    consequentialism, 58
    contractualism, 60
    deontology, 59
    existentialism, 61
    teleology, 59
    virtue, 60

exercises:
  1.1 getting to know your own values, 18
  2.1 attention and direction, 46
  2.2 link between attention and values, 49

wellness wheel, 115
  see also—frameworks
shadow design, 77
  see also—design

T

time
  importance of in self-care, 111
  boundaries and, 143
transitions, ix, 15, 165

U

unconscious design, 154, 191, 194
unintended consequences, xi, 30, 76
  see also—design

V

values, 1–25
  attention and, 5, 188
  characteristics of, 6–7
  definition of, 4
  ethics and, 70
  identity and, 164, 167
    personality, 164
  importance of, 14
    defining behaviours, 16
    defining standards, 16
    directing attention, 15
    directing priorities, 15
    informing meaning
    making, 17
  schwarz theory of basic values, 6, 10
    achievement, 10, 21
    benevolence, 11, 20
    conformity, 11, 21
    hedonism, 10, 21
    power, 10, 21
    security, 10, 21
    self-direction, 10, 20

spirituality, 11
stimulation, 10, 21
tradition, 11, 21
universal, 11, 20
summary, 19–20
values survey—the values
project, 8,19

W

wellness wheel, 114–5
  see also—frameworks

THIS HUMAN UNIVERSE

This work, while deep and contemplative, is only of benefit if it makes it out of your head and into the world. We have created an ecosystem of resources to provide scaffolding and support for you in this work. They are listed below for you to explore.

COMMUNITY

This human community—a community of liked-minded people sharing their experiences with *this human*. Everyone here is familiar with the content covered in the *this human* books and courses. It is a place to support each other and access free events, resources, tools and a bunch of wonderful people. Hosted on Mighty Networks. community.thishuman.com

COURSES

Design Character Course—hosted within the community site, you can apply to do the 8-week course that accompanies this book. This course is also an elective in the RMIT Masters of Design Futures. thishuman.com/design-character

COACHING

Coaching and mentoring—if you want to work with me directly on this material or anything relating to your career as a designer or leader, I would love to hear from you. You can do that by joining the community, or booking a call with me via my website. melissenova.com

CONTENT

This human worksheets and tools—within the community we have made all the exercises, tools and worksheets from both books available for download to assist you in your work. This also includes a downloadable index for the first book. Many of illustrations are also available for you to download and use, just for fun. community.thishuman.com

Or, you can access all of these by visiting thishuman.com